B. Vizars   Moh McEwen

69/2000

Northern Exposure

The Royal Air Force at work in Scotland

Berry Vissers & Mark McEwan

Squadron Prints

Northern Exposure

The Royal Air Force at work in Scotland

Published in 2008 by

Squadron Prints Ltd.

P.O. Box 1977, Arbroath, Angus, DD11 2WW, Scotland

ISBN 978-0-9512656-2-8

Photography by Berry Vissers & Mark McEwan
Words by Mark McEwan
Designed by Berry Vissers
Edited by Mark Ayton
Printed by Astute Print & Design, Forfar

Acknowledgements

In preparing this pictorial work we have had tremendous help and co-operation from the RAF as a whole and we owe them a huge debt of gratitude. We are particularly grateful to Gp Capt Pete Rochelle and Flt Lt Mark Still, both of 617 Squadron, for believing in this project from day one, and to Flt Lt Calum Law of 12 Squadron for his invaluable help on numerous occasions. We would also like to thank the following people who have kindly assisted us during the making of this book :

RAF Leuchars:
Air Cdre Clive Bairsto, Gp Capt Andy Bowen, Wg Cdr Pete Cracroft, Wg Cdr Dave Hazell, Sqn Ldr Bret Archer, Sqn Ldr Keith Block, Sqn Ldr Blythe Crawford, Sqn Ldr Rob Deboys, Sqn Ldr Sue Freeman, Sqn Ldr Dave Gourley, Sqn Ldr Steve Kilvington, Sqn Ldr Gareth Littlechild, Sqn Ldr Paul McCombie, Sqn Ldr Richard Moyes, Sqn Ldr Steve Ross, Sqn Ldr Derek Sington, Sqn Ldr Keith Wardlaw, Flt Lt John Booth, Flt Lt Neil Clark, Flt Lt Gary Cooper, Flt Lt Mark Cowan, Flt Lt Roy Macintyre, Flt Lt Matt Masters, Flt Lt Duncan McNiven, Flt Lt Russ Nash, Flt Lt Richard Pargeter, Flt Lt Rob Stewart, Flt Sgt Andy Budge, Ms Roz Clark, Ms Alison Mackenzie, Ms Jayne Taylor-Gaskell

RAF Lossiemouth:
Air Cdre Mark Roberts, Gp Capt Al Monkman, Wg Cdr David Cooper, Wg Cdr Adrian Frost, Wg Cdr James Linter, Wg Cdr Mike Saunders, Sqn Ldr Pete Beckett, Sqn Ldr Paul Crutchlow, Sqn Ldr Jon Greenhowe, Sqn Ldr David Knowles, Sqn Ldr Matt Lawrence, Sqn Ldr Jon Nixon, Sqn Ldr Stu Oliver, Sqn Ldr Andy Turk, Flt Lt Emmet Cox, Flt Lt Chris Docherty, Flt Lt Tony Griffiths, Flt Lt Mark Haley, Flt Lt Elle Hillard, Flt Lt James Milmine, Flt Lt Chris Pote, Flt Lt Stuart Wallace, Sgt Mark Bean

RAF Kinloss:
Gp Capt Jerry Kessell, Sqn Ldr Mark Faulds, Sqn Ldr Barry Neilson, Sqn Ldr Malcom Parsons, Sqn Ldr Duncan Sutherland, Flt Lt Drew Buxton, Flt Lt Craig Harding, Flt Lt Justin Owen, Flt Lt Rick Riley, Flt Lt Steve Worth, Flt Sgt Mick Morris, Sgt Deeble, Sgt Foster, Sgt Dave Womack, SAC Andy Hinton, CWO Richard Barker, FSC Grant Linklater, Ms Fiona Carle, Ms Hazel Lawson, Ms Dawn McNiven

RAF Kirknewton:
Sqn Ldr Allan Gillespie, Mr Graym Hunter

RM Condor:
Wg Cdr Lovat Fraser (Rtd), Sqn Ldr Bob Lyle

Glasgow International Airport:
Flt Lt Roger Moody, Flt Lt Andrew Mosson, APO Stuart Milne, Off Cdt Gavin Wilkie

Elsewhere:
Wg Cdr Darren Legg, Wg Cdr John Prescott, Sqn Ldr Graeme Bagnall, Sqn Ldr Brian Handy, Sqn Ldr Jez Holmes, Sqn Ldr Andy Pawsey, Lt Cdr Tank Murray, Lt Cdr Mike Wilkinson, Flt Lt Dan Ackroyd, Flt Lt Pete Griffiths, Flt Lt Jon Heywood, Flt Lt Phil Millward, Flt Lt Mark Pocock, Lt Angela Lewis, Mr Mark Ayton, Mr Alan Carlaw, Mr Martin Henshaw, Mr Bob Kemp, Mr Pete Kinsey, Mr Dougie Nicolson, Mr Roy Wilson, Ms Gillian Arnott, Ms Shaikha al Dhaheri, Ms Betty Howie, Ms Morag Nicol

Also not to be forgotten is 101 Squadron, RAF Brize Norton, the Visiting Aircraft Servicing Sections, Medical Sections and Life Support Sections at RAF Kinloss, RAF Leuchars and RAF Lossiemouth, plus the countless engineers, support and administrative staff behind the scenes. They have all done a fantastic job and we could not have produced this work without their help.

Squadron Prints

Air Commodore C A Bairsto

SAC Dolina Day / RAF Leuchars

Congratulations are due to the team from Squadron Prints who have done such a splendid job in producing this excellent record, in film and word, of the modern day Royal Air Force in Scotland.

I have been very lucky in a career spanning 30 years, and near on 3,000 flying hours, to have served three periods at Royal Air Force Leuchars in Scotland. Now, as Air Officer Scotland, I am the senior Combat Ready officer on flying duties in the RAF and get to see a great deal of Scottish military aviation, too. But, even I, was unprepared for the magnificent diversity and most unusual mixture of aviation photographs contained within these pages.

Whether a casual observer or a seasoned 'spotter', there is something of interest for all in this book. Northern Exposure shows the Royal Air Force in Scotland against the exquisite background of the nation's countryside and waters, backed up by some very illuminating vignettes by our people based here. It gives a real sense of the balance in drama of service life between the extraordinary and the mundane. Beyond that, it also shows the great capabilities and sheer extent of the Air Power residing beside the runways and military airstrips across Scotland. Our proud Scottish nation's aircraft are often an instrument of war, operating in a breath from the tactical to the strategic, whether in territorial waters or in intervention operations abroad. But they are also articles that reinforce peace in our daily lives bringing help to the vulnerable, location to those lost and opportunity to the young. This is all beautifully captured within, and I commend this book to all as an iconic photographic record of the Scottish Royal Air Force in its 90th Anniversary year.

C A Bairsto
Air Commodore
Station Commander RAF Leuchars and
Air Officer Scotland for the Royal Air Force

June 2008

Over the years, my job has given me the opportunity to meet many real-life heroes with amazing stories to tell about their experiences, both joyous and heart-breaking. I have also been fortunate enough to take part in many unusual events for the camera, but my most memorable moment took place in September 2006 when I was given the opportunity to fly in the back seat of a Tornado F3 from RAF Leuchars, on the eve of the base's spectacular air show.

Dougie Nicolson / D C Thomson

I had always wanted to be a fighter pilot when I was a child, and this really was the fulfilment of a life-long ambition. As a great admirer of anything aviation-related, I had often looked on in wonderment and excitement as these magnificent machines flew past my Perthshire home on training exercises. I had never dreamt that one day I too would be flying in a supersonic fighter jet over the Scottish countryside! The whole experience also gave me a great insight into the day-to-day running of an RAF station, supported by thousands of men and women carrying out, what was to them, their routine tasks.

Every day the men and women of the Royal Air Force in Scotland are on constant standby – whether it is serving on the Tornado F3 squadrons on Quick Reaction Alert at RAF Leuchars, defending the UK's airspace, RAF Lossiemouth's Tornado GR4 squadrons on duty in the Middle East in support of UK troops on the ground, the bright yellow Search and Rescue Sea King helicopters rushing to the aid of a vessel in distress in the North Sea, or the Nimrod MR2s from RAF Kinloss on a Search and Rescue tasking or, like their colleagues flying the Tornado GR4s, on duty in the Middle East helping to fight the war against global terrorism.

These are but a few examples of the RAF at work which we see regularly on our television screens and read about in the newspapers. There are however, countless other personnel who make up this valuable team, from air traffic controllers to aircraft engineers, the Mountain Rescue Teams to the staff manning the Aeronautical Rescue Coordination Centre – 24 hours a day, 7 days a week, our Royal Air Force are there for us, ready and willing to work alongside others for our benefit.

By buying this book you will be helping to support those who have served their country in the past, and at the same time it will give you a little more insight into the Royal Air Force at work in Scotland.

Lorraine Kelly

June 2008

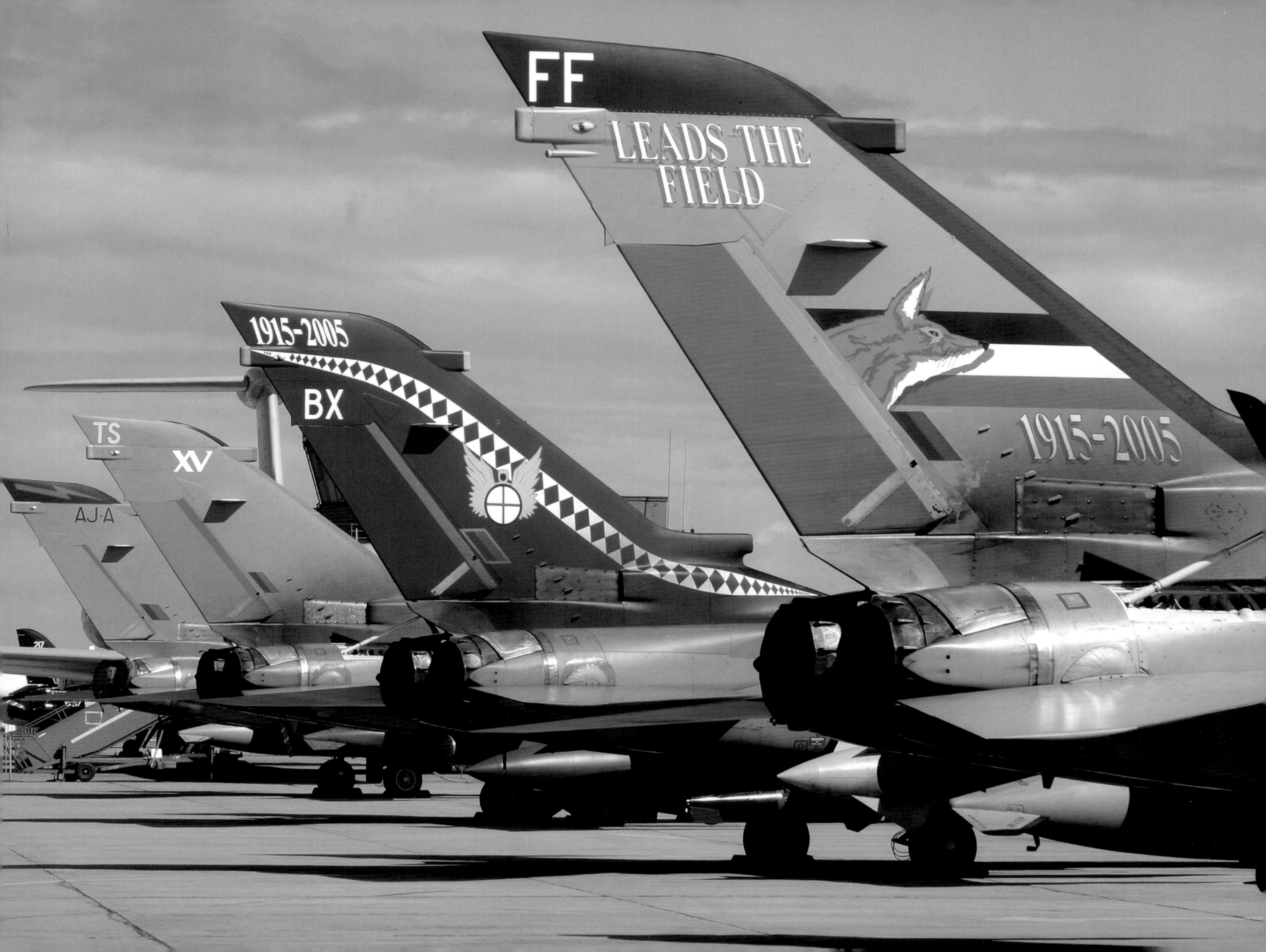

FF
LEADS THE FIELD
1915-2005
1915-2005
BX
TS
XV
AJ·A

This book was born out of many things – friendships, relationships, but most of all, a passion for aviation. For the authors, aviation has brought them much happiness and resulted in making some great friends along the way. Collectively, hundreds of hours have been spent during the making of this book, photographing man and machine at all levels, from the beginnings of training to the preparation for operational deployments, from the aircrew to the engineers, mountain rescue teams and administrative staff.

There are many units, squadrons and establishments within the RAF in Scotland, but with a finite period of time and space available, sacrifices had to be made in what could be covered. A decision therefore, was made to concentrate on only those squadrons operating aircraft. The authors would like to take this opportunity to pay tribute to all RAF personnel here in Scotland and beyond for their professionalism and commitment to serving their Country.

The decision to donate the proceeds of the book to the Royal Air Force Benevolent Fund was a very easy one to make. Berry's partner Gill Howie always speaks highly of her late father Alan, and about how much he loved his time in the RAF. Within two years of being diagnosed with Motor Neurone Disease in 1997, Alan was confined to the upstairs of his home in Arbroath. A chance remark to Air Commodore Jack Haines and his wife Lesley, at the RAF Leuchars Airshow, about the possibility of having a stair lift installed to improve his quality of life resulted in the RAF Benevolent Fund getting involved. Just five weeks later a stair lift had been installed at Alan's home. He was able to enjoy some freedom again and stayed fiercely proud of 'his' RAF until he passed away in 2001. 'Once RAF – always RAFBF!' is indeed true.

From the book's conception to its realisation, Mark's friend and Berry's partner Gill Howie has been there to provide encouragement and advice. In particular, the authors would like to thank Gill, without whom, this book would not have come to fruition.

Berry Vissers and Mark McEwan

June 2008

Operational Training

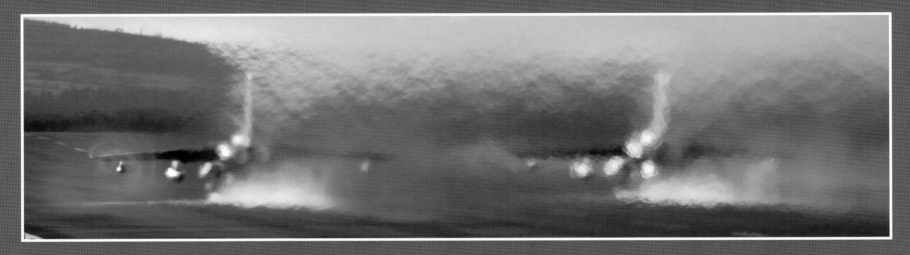

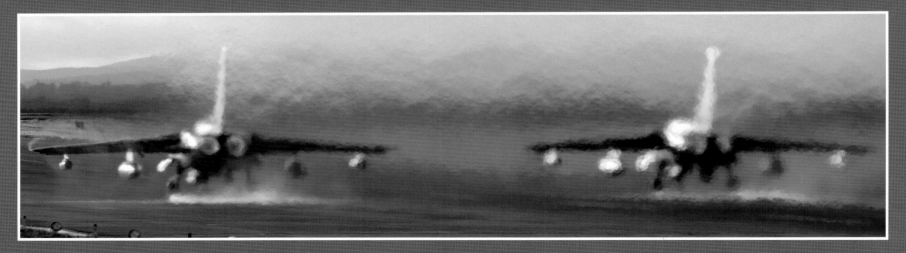

XV(Reserve) Squadron

Aim Sure

Base: RAF Lossiemouth, Moray   **Aircraft:** Tornado GR4

No. XV Squadron was formed on 1 March 1915 at South Farnborough, Hampshire. Initially equipped with BE 2Cs, the squadron deployed to France in December 1915 and undertook reconnaissance, bombing and Army co-operation duties on the Western Front. In February 1919, XV Squadron returned to the United Kingdom and disbanded at the end of that year. The squadron reformed in March 1924 as part of the Aeroplane & Armament Experimental Establishment (A&AEE) at Martlesham Heath, Suffolk. In June 1934 it moved to RAF Abingdon, Oxfordshire as a bomber unit flying Hawker Harts, which were superseded by Hinds in 1936 and Fairey Battles in 1938. In September 1939 the squadron deployed to France, but returned to England in December.

In November 1940 it received Wellingtons for night-bombing operations before converting to Stirlings five months later. Lady MacRobert presented one such aircraft to the squadron in memory of her three sons who were all killed in the air; the aircraft was named 'MacRobert's Reply'. No. XV Squadron flew Lancasters from 1943 and was part of the main force of Bomber Command for the rest of World War Two.

Based at RAF Wyton, Cambridgeshire from August 1946 the squadron received Lincolns in February 1947, Washingtons in January 1951 and Canberras in May 1953. In an unsettled period the squadron moved to Marham, Norfolk in 1950, Coningsby, Lincolnshire in 1951, Cottesmore, Rutland in 1954 and Honington, Suffolk in 1955. It then deployed to Cyprus in October 1956 in support of the Suez Campaign prior to disbanding on 15 April 1957. The squadron reformed with Victor B1s at Cottesmore on 1 September 1958 but disbanded once more on 31 October 1964. Remaining in retirement until 1 October 1970, XV Squadron reformed at RAF Honington with Buccaneer S2s before moving to RAF Laarbruch, West Germany on 11 January 1971.

On 31 October 1983 it became the first RAF Germany unit to receive Tornado GR1s. Using these aircraft the squadron played a major role in the Gulf War in 1991 for which it received its latest Battle Honour. The squadron disbanded on 18 December 1991 but was reformed with reserve status on 1 April 1992 to carry out the training task previously performed by the Tornado Weapons Conversion Unit based at RAF Honington. No. XV(R) Squadron moved to RAF Lossiemouth, Moray on 1 November 1993 and in March 1999 absorbed the RAF elements of the Tri-National Tornado Training Establishment from Cottesmore. The squadron converted to the Tornado GR4 in 2001 and is now responsible for training all Royal Air Force Tornado GR4 crews before they proceed to the front line. No. XV(R) Squadron continues to bear the MacRobert's coat of arms on the aircraft allocated the tail letter 'Foxtrot'. The current aircraft bearing the 'MacRobert's Reply' coat of arms is Tornado GR4 ZA459.

Gorse - During the spring and summer months, aircrew on approach to Lossiemouth's Runway 23 are welcomed by the sight of the golden blossom on the gorse bushes on the adjoining golf course.

Opposite

Flightline - *Responsible for training all pilots and weapon systems officers (WSOs) selected to fly the Tornado GR4, XV(R) Squadron is the Operational Conversion Unit (OCU) for the type. The unit is one of the biggest squadrons in the RAF with 26 aircraft on strength, and almost 50 instructor aircrew. Here the all-instructor aircrew complete their post-flight cockpit checks after returning from an exercise at RAF St Mawgan in Cornwall.*

Time - It takes around six months to train a Tornado GR4 pilot and WSO. After a month of ground school, ab initio crews are initially taught general handling, instrument flying, formation flying and basic weaponeering, before moving onto the advanced phase of the main conversion course which includes tactical flying, night flying and close air support training.

Retract - *Captured just as the undercarriage is completing its retraction cycle, callsign 'Mentor 1 & 2' perform a pairs take-off. For operational reasons, Tornado GR4s regularly transfer between the eight squadrons, and as illustrated here, the aircraft furthest from the camera wears the markings of RAF Marham-based 31 Squadron.*

Velocity *- The backbone of the RAF's strike capability, the Panavia Tornado GR4 is a considerably more advanced offensive platform than its original incarnation as the Tornado GR1. Seen here in its element, the Tornado was originally designed to penetrate deep into enemy airspace below the cover of radar, but it has proved its worth in a variety of roles since it was first delivered in 1982, and is capable of carrying a formidable arsenal of weapons.*

Tanking - As part of the formation flying phase of the six-month Tornado GR4 conversion course, two sorties will involve Air-to-Air Refuelling (AAR). Here, the closest jet of the two-ship formation has its refuelling probe out ready to plug in behind the tanker.

Twist - The squadron has around 250 engineers, and like other Tornado units, day-to-day aircraft rectification tasks are carried out at squadron level. Here engineers are removing the inboard pylon from the starboard wing in XV(R) Squadron's cavernous maintenance hangar.

Above

Fix - Engineers work on an engine snag, in this case, a problem with the afterburner on the port engine. After the snag is fixed, the aircraft will undergo engine runs in the test bay prior to being declared serviceable.

Detune - About to undergo engine tests in the detuner. The red engine intake protection grilles ensure that the risk of Foreign Object Damage (FOD) is minimised during the engine runs.

Adrenaline *- Night flying is bread and butter work for Tornado GR4 crews, and its importance is underlined during the night phase of the conversion course. Crews will not only be expected to fly at low-level at night, but also undertake sorties as part of a two, three and four-ship formations.*

56(Reserve) Squadron

Quid si cœlum ruat - *What if heaven falls?*

No. 56 Squadron formed at Gosport, Hampshire on 9 June 1916 and flew a variety of aircraft before moving to France in April 1917 with SE 5s. For the remainder of World War One the squadron flew patrols over the Western Front. Several famous Royal Flying Corps pilots served with the squadron, including founder member Captain Albert Ball, who was killed in action on 7 May 1917 and was posthumously awarded the Victoria Cross (VC). Captain James McCudden was another recipent of the VC, with 57 victories to his name. By the time the war ended, the squadron had claimed no less than 427 victories. It returned to England in December 1919, disbanding on 22 January 1920. Only 12 days later, on 1 February 1920, 56 Squadron re-appeared in Egypt equipped with Snipes, but disbanded again on 23 September 1922. The squadron reformed at Hawkinge, Kent on 1 November 1922 and was equipped successively with Snipes, Grebes, Siskins, Bulldogs, Gauntlets and Gladiators.

Receiving Hurricanes at North Weald, Essex in May 1938, the squadron was detached to France in May 1940 before taking part in the Battle of Britain. Typhoons were delivered in September 1941 and the squadron was the first to fly this type on ground-attack and anti-shipping missions. Spitfires were flown from April until June 1944 when it re-equipped with Tempest Vs, these aircraft being used to good effect against V1 flying bombs over Southern England. The squadron moved to Belgium in September 1944 and, for the remainder of the war, was engaged in armed reconnaissance sweeps over Germany.

Returning to England on 1 April 1946, 56 Squadron was equipped with Meteor F3s but these, in turn, were replaced with Meteor F4s, Meteor F8s, Swifts, Hunters and Lightnings, with which type the squadron formed 'The Firebirds' aerobatic team. After a period in Cyprus as part of the Near East Air Force, the squadron returned to the United Kingdom in July 1976 to re-equip with the Phantom FGR2 at RAF Wattisham, Suffolk as part of the UK Air Defence Force. Here it served with some distinction for the remainder of the Cold War, winning the Dacre Trophy four times as best Air Defence squadron. The squadron was disbanded on 1 July 1992 as a result of the 'Options For Change' defence review. Simultaneously it reformed as a 'shadow' squadron when it moved to RAF Coningsby, Lincolnshire, to become the Tornado F3 Operational Conversion Unit as 56(Reserve) Squadron.

The squadron then moved to RAF Leuchars, Fife, in April 2003, where it was responsible for training Tornado F3 pilots and navigators. It was also the Tornado F3 force standards evaluation unit and the squadron ran the Tornado F3 Qualified Weapons Instructors (QWI) course until its disbandment on 22 April, 2008. According to legend, 'the Phoenix will rise from the ashes', and 56(R) Squadron reformed again at RAF Waddington as the ISTAR OEU (Intelligence, Surveillance, Target Acquisition and Reconnaissance Operational Evaluation Unit).

Phoenix - For the 2005 air show display season, 56(R) Squadron marked up five Tornado F3s with a special red flash and 'Firebirds 2005' insignia. Flown by pilot Flt Lt Richard 'Dicko' Moyes and weapon systems officer Flt Lt Gareth 'Gaz' Littlechild, the crew had over 2,500 flying hours in the Tornado F3 between them.

Whip - *Forming up in a diamond nine, callsign 'Phoenix 4' (centre right) closes in on the rest of the formation over the East coast of Scotland. The 'whip' aircraft, in this case another Tornado F3, is present to assist the nine crews in keeping formation, and can be seen above the formation.*

Opposite
Flyover - *June 2006 marked the 90th Anniversary of 56 Squadron, and as part of the celebrations, the squadron carried out a nine-ship flypast of the Forth Bridges. This event was repeated more recently in April 2008 when the squadron disbanded . On both occasions, the ground crew worked extremely hard and the start-up of the jets went without a hitch. It was an impressive sight to see so many aircraft getting airborne at the same time. Two of the Scottish landmarks 'visited' during the event in 2006 were the Forth Rail and Road Bridges connecting Edinburgh with the Kingdom of Fife and the Tay Bridge. It would have taken a car about 50 minutes to drive from one bridge to the other, whilst the Tornados did this in only nine minutes - and this was with a detour around St Andrews and a flypast at RAF Leuchars!*

Farewell - *To mark the end of fighter operations for 56(Reserve) Squadron, a commemorative flypast around Scotland took place on 18 April 2008. Led by the Firebirds' boss Wing Commander Dave 'Nutty' Hazell, the formation over-flew some of the airfields and airports which had worked closely with the squadron during its five-year tenure at RAF Leuchars. This image shows the formation flying over Aberdeen Airport, the terminal and some of the stands being clearly visible below.*

Fireworks *- A timed exposure of part of 56(R) Squadron's flightline
captures a Tornado F3's afterburner trail as the aircraft gets airborne.*

Flame - *The front undercarriage just begins to lift here as 'Tango Oscar' races down the RAF Kinloss runway in full afterburner. During the summer of 2007, the squadron 'bolt-holed' to the Moray base while RAF Leuchars underwent major runway and taxiway resurfacing work.*

Care - Groundcrew prepare the jets for the following day's flying programme. Until its disbandment on April 22, 2008, the 'Firebirds' operated a fleet of 14 aircraft that were maintained by a team of around 190 tradesmen carrying out routine maintenance and rectification tasks when required.

Flight Sergeant Andy Budge explains the role of the engineers on 56(R) Squadron.

"Combat aircraft are highly complex pieces of equipment and they require a team of skilled engineers to keep them flying. A team of some 190 tradesmen undertake all the routine maintenance and rectification tasks associated with the squadron's demanding flying programme. The engineers operate as two identical shifts, on alternating day and night shift patterns. The day shift starts at 07:30 and finishes at 16:30, when the night shift commences, lasting until approximately 02:00 the following morning.

The engineers' efforts are split into two areas; flight line operations and rectification tasks. The flight line (known as the line) tasks cover the servicing required to prepare the aircraft for flight, and then the launch and subsequent recovery procedures. Prior to a sortie, the 'lineys', as they are known, check fluid levels, tyre pressures and liquid oxygen (LOX) content. They then perform a thorough visual inspection of the aircraft.

When the aircrew arrive at their jet, the lineys help them to strap in to their ejector seats. Once 'strapping-in' is complete the lineys carry out the 'see-off' procedure to enable the aircraft to get airborne."

Nightshift - A squadron engineer makes light work of a 1500 litre (330 gallon) fuel tank carried on a weapons load trolley.

"Ninety minutes, and a cup of tea later, the lineys see the aircraft back in, service it and get it ready for the next sortie. The line consists of approximately 20 personnel. Flight line personnel are often the members of a squadron seen by the public when working on the line, either at the home station or during an airshow. As such they represent the public face of the unit, but also play a vital role in achieving the training schedule of a busy Operational Conversion Unit.

The remaining engineers carry out a myriad of rectification tasks associated with maintaining a fleet of 14 Tornado F3 aircraft. There are two types of tasks: repair of faults reported by the aircrew following a sortie, and routine servicing. Faults reported by the aircrew following a sortie require in-depth diagnosis, normally followed by component replacement, and then a series of functional tests. Routine servicing consists of inspections and scheduled component replacements that have to be carried out to ensure the aircraft remains safe to operate. All rectification tasks are carried out in strict accordance with detailed procedures to ensure the safety of the crew and aircraft at all times.

All engineers are highly trained and work within three trade groups. 'Mechanical' deal with the propulsion and airframe systems, the engines, flying controls, undercarriage and environmental systems. 'Avionics' deal with electrical and avionics systems, including the radios, radar, navigational kit and the weapons control systems. 'Weapons' are responsible for the offensive and defensive armament devices and the aircraft assisted escape systems. All three groups work as a single team to meet the challenging engineering requirements of the squadron's flying task. Overcoming such challenges is all the more satisfying on special occasions when the squadron may perform a diamond nine formation flypast, then all the hard work and effort is more than worthwhile!"

Lethal - The nose cone of the Tornado F3 houses the long range AI.24 Foxhunter radar. Originally produced by GEC-Marconi, the radar enables the aircraft to engage targets well beyond visual range.

Rainbow - A spectacular ending to the Tornado F3 solo display provided by 56(R) Squadron at the annual air show at Leuchars. This phenomenon was created by a combination of high speed and the atmospheric conditions on the day.

Homeward - The diamond nine in the turn over the South bank of the River Tay as they head back home towards Leuchars.

42(Reserve) Squadron

Fortiter in re - *Bravely into action*

Base: RAF Kinloss, Moray   **Aircraft:** Nimrod MR2

Spey - *Powered by four Rolls-Royce Spey Mk250 turbofan engines, XV245 demonstrates the Nimrod MR2's impressive low-speed handling capabilities.*

No. 42 Squadron formed at Filton, Avon, on 1 April 1916 and moved to France in August with BE 2D and BE 2E aircraft to undertake the reconnaissance role. In April 1917 it re-equipped with RE8s and moved to Northern Italy to cover the Austro-Italian Front, returning to France in March 1918. In February 1919 it returned to the United Kingdom and disbanded at Netheravon, Hampshire, on 26 June 1919.

No. 42 Squadron reformed at Donibristle, Fife, on 14 December 1936 from 'B' Flight of No. 22 Squadron equipped with Vildebeasts as one of the only two torpedo strike units in the United Kingdom. The squadron relocated to RAF Bircham Newton, Norfolk, on 12 August 1939 where it exchanged its Vildebeasts for Beauforts in April 1940, specialising in anti-shipping and mine laying along the coasts of Northern Europe. On 18 June 1942 it departed the United Kingdom for the Far East but delayed in the Middle East, finally arriving in Ceylon in December. It converted to Blenheim Vs in India, which where used for bombing missions over Burma from March 1943 but re-equipped with Hurricane IICs in October for ground-attack duties, adding Mk IVs in November 1944. A change to Thunderbolt IIs took place in July 1945, before disbanding at Meiktala in Burma on 30 December, that year. It reformed with Beaufighter Xs at Thorney Island, Essex on 1 October 1946 as part of Coastal Command's Strike Wing, but disbanded again on 15 October 1947.

The squadron reformed at St Eval in Cornwall on 28 June 1952 with Shackleton MR1s for maritime reconnaissance duties. Shackleton MR2s were received in April 1954 and the squadron moved to RAF St Mawgan, Cornwall, on 8 October 1958, where MR3s were accepted in December 1965. It converted to the Nimrod MR1 in April 1971 and received MR2s in 1983. In April 1982 it dispatched two aircraft to Ascension Island as part of the Falklands Campaign and in October 1990 it detached crews to Oman as part of Operation GRANBY. Disbanded as a front line unit on 1 October 1992, the 42 Squadron number-plate continues as the Nimrod Operational Conversion Unit. Today, the squadron is responsible for training all RAF Nimrod crews and it will be the first squadron to convert to the Nimrod MRA4 in 2009.

Conversion - *No. 42(Reserve) Squadron is the Operational Conversion Unit (OCU) for the Nimrod MR2 and is responsible for crew conversion onto the type. It takes approximately eight months to train ab initio students on the Nimrod long course, with pilots, flight engineers and weapon systems operators (WSOps) staying together as a crew for its duration. On completion, they leave the OCU qualified as limited Combat Ready Standard (CRS) and join either of the two frontline squadrons based at RAF Kinloss. All crew gain full proficiency on the type with a frontline squadron.*

Wingtips - *The Nimrod MR2 carries a LORAL Electronic Support Measures (ESM) pod on each wingtip. Fitted to the fleet during the mid-1980s, the equipment provides warning analysis of hostile radar.*

Stores - *Several Nimrod MR2s have been modified to carry BOZ-107 chaff and flare dispensers on both the port and starboard stores pylons – initially employed on the aircraft during the Gulf War in 1991, as well as a FLIR (Forward Looking Infrared) turret below the starboard wing.*

Replacement - Set to replace the existing Nimrod MR2 fleet from 2009 onwards are twelve BAe Systems Nimrod MRA4s. Although the new aircraft are manufactured using surplus Nimrod fuselages, the MRA4 differs vastly from its predecessor, both in looks and capability. The design includes new Rolls-Royce BR710 engines – 25% more powerful and yet 30% more efficient than the Spey Mk250, larger wings, plus a new bomb bay and undercarriage, as well as a Tactical Command System (TCS).

Future - No. 42(R) Squadron is at the heart of the Nimrod MRA4's introduction into RAF service, and will provide the first crews to convert onto the type. The new aircraft has a state-of-the-art glass cockpit, which utilises many of the features used by Airbus in its airliner cockpits. MRA4 crew will comprise a pilot and co-pilot plus eight-mission crewmembers who will operate the TCS. On-board sensors include the new high-performance Thales Searchwater 2000MR multi-mode all-weather search radar. Once introduced, the MRA4 will continue to operate in the traditional roles undertaken by the MR2 including Anti-Submarine Warfare (ASW), Search And Rescue (SAR) as well as facing the new challenges of global terrorism.

Front Line

12(Bomber) Squadron

Leads the field

Base: RAF Lossiemouth, Moray   **Aircraft:** Tornado GR4

Formed at Netheravon, Hampshire on 14 February 1915, 12 Squadron moved to St Omer in France in September equipped with BE 2Cs. From early 1916 the squadron confined its activities to reconnaissance and re-equipped with BE 2Es. After the Armistice the squadron moved to Germany with the Army of Occupation until disbanding at Bickendorf on 22 July 1922.

No. 12(B) reformed as a bomber squadron at RAF Northolt, Middlesex on 1 April 1923 equipped with DH 9As. These were soon replaced by Fawns, which in turn, gave way to Foxes, Harts and Hinds. The squadron moved to Andover, Hampshire in March 1924 and moved to Aden in October 1935 for ten months. The squadron deployed to France at the outbreak of World War Two. During this difficult time, Flying Officer D.E. Garland and Sergeant T. Gray were each posthumously awarded the Victoria Cross for their efforts in stemming the enemy advance.

Back in England the squadron continued attacks on Channel Ports and re-armed with Wellingtons in October 1940. Lancasters were received in November 1942 and were retained until the arrival of Lincolns in August 1946. Canberra B2s were taken on strength in April 1952, but these were replaced by B6s in May 1955, being flown in the Suez Campaign in 1956 from Malta. After returning to RAF Binbrook, Lincolnshire, the squadron moved to RAF Coningsby, Lincolnshire, where it disbanded on 13 July 1961. It reformed there on 1 July 1962 flying the Vulcan B2 but stood down on 31 December 1967.

The squadron reformed at RAF Honington, Suffolk, on 1 October 1969 as the RAF's first Buccaneer maritime strike squadron and moved to RAF Lossiemouth, Moray in October 1980. The Buccaneers were used to good effect during the Gulf Conflict in 1991 where they provided designation for laser-guided bombs. No. 12(B) Squadron re-equipped with Tornado GR1s on 1 October 1993 retaining its maritime strike commitment. In December 1998 the squadron was back in the Gulf employing the GR1 with skill and accuracy during the aptly named Operation DESERT FOX. The squadron upgraded to the Tornado GR4 in 1999 and became precision-guided munitions specialists. In 2003, 12(B) Squadron saw action over the skies of Iraq and, whilst flying from Al Udeid AB, Qatar, led the RAF's involvement in Operation TELIC. In January 2005, during the Squadron's 90th year, the aircraft were again patrolling the skies over Iraq during the country's first free elections for over 50 years. No. 12 Squadron continues to support our troops in the Gulf and will 'Lead the Field' in future operations around the globe.

Fire - *A fiery sky provides a dramatic backdrop to this 12 Squadron Tornado GR4 as it taxies off Lossiemouth's active runway at dusk.*

Plans - Mission planning is an essential task before each sortie. Here 12 Squadron aircrew map out their intended low level routing, for a morning mission from RAF Lossiemouth.

Walk - After receiving an 'out brief', the pilot and weapon systems officer walk to the Hardened Aircraft Shelter (HAS) where their allocated jet is parked ready for the sortie. No.12 Squadron has nine such shelters in its complex, each normally containing a single Tornado GR4. Designed and constructed during the Cold War as a means of protecting aircraft from an indirect nuclear strike, the value of HAS operations has been eroded by the advent of precision-guided munitions and the enemy's ability to strike a HAS with relative ease.

Probe - *No.12 Squadron has an unwritten rule that all of its aircraft should taxi back to the squadron HAS site with the air-to-air refuelling probe and air brakes deployed. This allows ground crew to inspect the probe for possible damage after an air-to-air refuelling sortie, and to conduct a better pre-flight inspection of each component. The probe can only be retracted hydraulically and remains deployed until the aircraft has hydraulic power when started. Some personnel claim that the real reason for taxiing in with the airbrakes deployed is because they look like the ears of the 12 Squadron fox!*

HUD - *Green in colour, the Head-Up Display (HUD) stands out well as this Tornado GR4 emerges from its shelter. The aircraft is carrying a TIALD targeting pod and a Carrier Bomb Light Store pod on the underbelly pylons.*

Below
Eyeball - What has caught this WSO's eye as his aircraft holds prior to departure? Another Tornado GR4 breaking into the circuit? An airliner high over the top? Or perhaps he's rehearsing the next sortie in his head?

Lead - This sequence of shots illustrates the final signals given by the pilot of the lead aircraft to his wingman during a pairs take-off. The pilot taps his forehead three times with his hand, tilts his head back in an over-exaggerated fashion and pauses briefly, then leans forward to signal 'brakes off'. The pilot uses the three forehead taps to ensure the wingman is aware that 'brakes off' signal is imminent.

Alarm *- Carrying a single ALARM (Air Launched Anti-Radiation Missile) on the starboard under-belly pylon, this Tornado GR4 commences its take-off run from Lossie's Runway 23. Manufactured by MBDA, the missile is designed to destroy or suppress enemy ground-based radar systems.*

Paveway - Enhanced Paveway III has a modified guidance section and wiring to accommodate a Global Positioning System Aided Inertial Navigation System (GAINS). This weapon is the latest version of the Paveway family of laser-guided bombs within the Tornado GR4 arsenal. No.12 Squadron is the RAF's lead Tornado GR4 unit for Paveway, as well as the lead Lossiemouth unit for ALARM.

Trail - *The RAF's frontline fast jets regularly deploy to the United States on exercise. Getting them there is no mean feat, requiring several support aircraft, including airborne tanker aircraft such as the VC-10 or as illustrated here, one of the RAF's Lockheed Tristar fleet about to refuel a Tornado GR4 on an Easterly trail home.*

Flight Lieutenant Chris Pote recalls his first air-to-air refuelling sortie.

"Air-to-air refuelling is a critical force multiplier in any modern, flexible air force, allowing greater time on task and longer ranges to be covered. It is a skill that any fast jet pilot has to master, day or night and sometimes in poor weather – as if precise formation on an airliner isn't hard enough!

Today was my introduction to the challenge, to refuel from one of the RAF's Tristars over the North Sea. The day started with a comprehensive brief from the instructor who would be sitting eight feet behind me, keeping the proceedings safe. It is important that standard procedures are followed throughout. You join on the left, moving forward so that the tanker pilot can see you. When ready to refuel, you move backwards and down until you are behind the hose, then move across to wait about six feet behind the basket. It is important to minimise the tanker crews' grey hairs, not to have a closing vector on the tanker, apart from the very last few feet. Once stabilised in the waiting position, you move forward, keeping steady, looking at the refuelling unit, whilst listening to directions from the weapon systems officer. That's the theory, now for the practice!

We climbed out from Berwick-upon-Tweed after a fast moving 2 vs 1 sortie – time to forget about trying to shoot the bad guys and to think about the next challenge. Some deft radar work from the rear-seat pilot found the tanker 30 miles away and we planned our intercept. My first impression was the sheer size. Then I moved in underneath its belly – the world became dark as I moved up and forwards. It was as if I was standing underneath the aeroplane on the ground, possibly closer. My first attempt resulted in the basket gracefully pirouetting around the probe, scuffing the fuselage side, as I ran out of momentum at the critical moment. The embarrassing call of "rim, no damage" came from the rear seat. Oh well, try again. Try as I might the knuckles of my right hand went white, as if I was trying to squeeze the stick to death. Come on, relax, as I put the left engine into minimum reheat to counter the massive downwash below the 200 tonne airliner. This time, I took my eyes off the references and tried to cheat, looking at the basket – it all went wrong, the basket moved, I moved and we began a clumsy dance with awful timing – back off and let it stabilise. Having settled down, I moved forwards again, this time listening to the calm instructions from the rear seat "slightly up, slightly right, push, contact". Push the hose in to the markings, the green light comes on and for the first time in my life, the fuel gauge is showing the quantity increasing whilst airborne. Phew!"

Finals - Very short finals over the lights to land on Lossie's Runway 05 in late afternoon sunshine.

14 Squadron

أنا أصف و أفي - *I spread my wings and keep my promise*

Base: RAF Lossiemouth, Moray   **Aircraft:** Tornado GR4

No. 14 Squadron formed at Shoreham, Sussex on 3 February 1915. Equipped with BE 2s, the squadron moved to Egypt for Army co-operation duties in the Middle East. It served in Palestine, Arabia and the Western Desert, before returning to the United Kingdom in January 1919 where it disbanded the following month. A year later, on 1 February 1920, 111 Squadron was re-numbered to 14 Squadron - quite appropriate considering 111 Squadron was formed from a flight of 14 Squadron!

Over the next 20 years, the squadron patrolled Transjordan and Palestine and during that time the unit gained its Arabic motto. During World War Two, 14 Squadron remained in the Middle East, only to return to the United Kingdom on 24 October 1944. Based at Chivenor, Devon the squadron re-equipped with Wellington XIVs until it disbanded on 25 May 1945. On the same day, 143 Squadron at Banff, Scotland, was re-numbered 14 Squadron and moved to Cambrai, France, six months later, only to be disbanded again on 31 March 1946. However, the following day, 128 Squadron at Wahn, West Germany, was re-numbered to 14 Squadron, thus continuing the squadron's existence. After various re-locations in West Germany, the squadron disbanded at RAF Gütersloh on 17 December 1962.

Continuation of the 14 Squadron number-plate was secured the same day by the re-numbering of Canberra B(I)8-equipped 88 Squadron based at RAF Wildenrath. No. 14 Squadron flew these Canberras from Wildenrath until it re-located to Brüggen, West Germany, in June 1970. Equipped initially with Phantom FGR2s, the squadron received Jaguar GR1s in April 1975 and Tornado GR1s in November 1985. In August 1990, in response to Iraq's invasion of Kuwait, personnel and aircraft from 14 Squadron deployed to the Middle East as part of the Allied Coalition Forces. The squadron returned to the Middle East on a regular basis to enforce the safe policing of the Southern Iraqi no-fly zones. In April 1999, in response to Serbian aggression in Kosovo, the squadron mounted air strikes from RAF Brüggen during Operation ENGADINE as part of the Allied Coalition Force against the Serbian military infrastructure both in Kosovo and Serbia.

The Squadron re-located from RAF Brüggen to RAF Lossiemouth, Moray, in January 2001 where it continues to operate the Tornado GR4. No. 14 Squadron is the Tornado GR4 Force lead unit in targeting pods and precision-guided munitions. It utilises a number of weapon systems that includes, the ULTRA/RAFAEL LITENING III targeting pod and the SELEX Thermal Imaging Airborne Laser Designator (TIALD) pod, in conjunction with GPS and laser-guided weapons. On 1 February 2007, 14 Squadron became the first RAF unit to use LITENING III in combat over Iraq while deployed in support of Operation TELIC.

Underside - This underbelly shot of a Tornado GR4 illustrates the aircraft's variable geometry wings fully swept at 67 degrees. The aircraft is pictured carrying three 1,500 litre (330 gallon) fuel tanks, two BOZ-107 chaff and flare dispenser pods, and a carrier bomb light store (CBLS) with four 3kg (6.6lb) practice bombs.

Home - *Unmistakably Lossie! 'Bravo Charlie' on short finals for Runway 23, with the Covesea Lighthouse in the background - a familiar sight around the Moray Basin.*

Flight Lieutenant James Milmine, a Tornado GR4 pilot, explains the pre-flight procedures carried out prior to a sortie.

"Following an operations briefing, I receive a detailed brief from the squadron engineers on the aircraft's state and also scrutinize its logbook, called the Form 700. The logbook contains records of the aircraft's various modifications, limitations and service history. With one critical signature I take charge of the aircraft, worth around £40 million. From that point onwards I am responsible for anything that happens to it until I return to the rectification control room and sign it back over to the engineers at the end of the sortie.

By the time I get to the aircraft the weapon systems officer (WSO) is already strapped in and busy loading mission data into the main computer and bringing the navigation and weapon systems online. Although the aircraft has been thoroughly checked over by the engineers, as the captain I have to perform another thorough check before the flight, known as 'the walkround'.

No matter how complex the sortie, the captain will always perform this check, often with one of the engineers by his side. It is the last chance to spot a loose panel or a flat tyre. When we are on operations and carrying live weapons it is also an opportunity for the aircrew to check that the weapons are fit for flight; in this case the WSO will join me and we will run through the checks strictly from the flight reference cards."

Pre-flight - *A 14 Squadron pilot performs the all-important pre-flight walkaround, while the groundcrew, or 'lineys' carry out their duties prior to the sortie.*

Assist - A 'liney' assists a pilot strapping into a Martin-Baker Mk10A zero/zero ejection seat.

"Once I'm satisfied with the state of the aircraft I'll check my ejection seat. Hopefully, I will not need to use it, but if I do, I want to make sure it will work, and once again there is a strict list of checks to ensure this! 'Strapping-in' is done with the help of the 'liney' (an engineer) assisting our 'see-off'. There are many straps and restraints that hold you into the seat, not to mention tubes and cabling for the communications, oxygen and the anti-g system.

The liney will then stand in front of the aircraft and talk to the pilot on the headset to complete the process of starting the jet. One of the checks is to make sure all the control surfaces of the aircraft work properly. For example, when I pull the stick backwards (to increase height) the horizontal tails would need to travel down. The liney will check visually that this does indeed happen. Their role and dedication is critical to ensure that the aircraft gets airborne and returns safely."

Hotpit - In an effort to increase squadron sortie rates without increasing maintenance hours, Tornado GR4s are hot-refuelled. The right engine is shut down and while refuelling takes place, one crew swaps for another and a follow-on sortie is flown. This allows each aircraft to carry out three sorties in one day rather than the usual two, serviceability permitting.

Office - It's not everyone who has this view from their office window! A fisheye lens adds to the distortion of the aircraft canopy to create this unusual fly-on-the-wall image.

Crusader - *Crystal clear Scottish winter light brilliantly illuminates the underside of 'Bravo X-ray' as it banks hard over the Scottish Highlands.*

Opposite
Talkdown - *With gear and flaps in the lowered position, callsign 'Snake 1 & 2' carry out a pairs radar approach to Lossie's Runway 23 over the Moray Basin.*

Tranquility - *The warm glow of the setting sun belies the icy, but unusually calm North Sea in early winter.*

617 Squadron

Après moi, le déluge - *After me, the flood*

Base: RAF Lossiemouth, Moray   **Aircraft:** Tornado GR4

No. 617 Squadron formed at RAF Scampton, Lincolnshire, on 21 March 1943, for the special task of breaching the Möhne, Eder and Sorpe dams by the use of the now legendary Wallis 'bouncing bombs'. The squadron was equipped with the modified Lancaster B III (Special). Its first leader, Wing Commander G P Gibson DSO DFC, was awarded the Victoria Cross for his gallantry during the attack. After the raid it was decided to retain the squadron for other special operations and it went on to deliver weapons like the 12,000lb (5,443kg) 'Tallboy' and 22,000lb (9,950kg) 'Grand Slam' bombs.

Staying in Lincolnshire, the squadron later operated from RAF Coningsby and RAF Woodhall Spa, moving to RAF Waddington, in June 1945 and disbanded at RAF Binbrook on 15 December 1955. On 1 May 1958 the 'Dambusters' reformed at RAF Scampton with Vulcan B1s as part of the RAF's V-bomber force. In September 1961 it re-equipped with the Vulcan B2, which was modified to carry the Blue Steel 'stand-off' bomb. The squadron continued in the long-range bombing role until disbanding on 31 December 1981.

For its third life it reformed as a strike squadron at RAF Marham, Norfolk, on 1 January 1983, flying the Tornado GR1. During the Gulf War in 1991 the squadron flew in its established role but also pioneered the use of the new Thermal Imaging Airborne Laser Designator (TIALD) pod. In 1992 the squadron was deployed to the Gulf for Operation JURAL as part of the UN force monitoring the 'no-fly' zone in Southern Iraq.

In April 1994, 617 Squadron added maritime strike to its list of specialist skills and moved to RAF Lossiemouth, Moray, re-equipped with Tornado GR1Bs. Between 1995 and 1998, the squadron deployed to Turkey and Saudi Arabia for Operations WARDEN and JURAL, monitoring the 'no-fly' zones in Northern and Southern Iraq. Since 1999, the squadron has continued in this role, operating from Ali Al Salem Air Base in Kuwait supporting Operations BOLTON and RESINATE SOUTH, during which it flew reconnaissance missions and attacked targets in Iraq employing laser-guided bombs. The 'Dambusters' currently operate the Tornado GR4, with enhanced night capability and the use of advanced weapons such as Storm Shadow. The squadron introduced this precision attack stand-off cruise missile during Operation TELIC. Air and ground crew feel proud in being part of this prestigious unit and to commemorate this, some Tornado GR4s are decorated with identification codes as worn during the bombing raids in World War Two.

Starbound - *No. 617 Squadron is the youngest operational frontline squadron in the RAF today, and is almost certainly the most famous. The squadron is one of four Tornado GR4 units which make up RAF Lossiemouth's 140 Expeditionary Air Wing.*

Burner - Tornado GR4 ZG727/AJ-J, radio callsign 'Gibson 1' departs from Lossie's Runway 23 at low-level, looking dramatic in full afterburner.

Opposite
Storm Shadow - Tornado GR4 aircrew from 617 Squadron were the first to use the Storm Shadow long-range stand-off missile operationally during Operation TELIC over Iraq in 2003.

Raw - Brakes off and full power selected, this Tornado GR4 will be airborne in a matter of seconds bound for the nearby bombing range at RAF Tain, Ross-shire.

Frontline - *Restrained to his Martin-Baker Mk10A ejection seat, and wearing immersion suit, g-suit and life saving jacket (LSJ), the pilot begins the start-up procedure for the Tornado GR4. Note the clear plastic thigh pockets of his flight suit, which contain briefing notes and charts for the sortie. The cover of his helmet visor is adorned with red 617 Squadron lightning flashes.*

Flight Lieutenant Mark Still shares his experience as a weapon systems officer in a Tornado GR4 during an operational mission.

"Often when we fly training sorties over the bombing ranges in the North of Scotland, we drop weapons, whether they are practice, dumb or precision-guided. Yet, when we carry live weapons in an operational theatre and are tasked to destroy a real target, all the training in the world cannot prevent us from feeling nervous. We have to fall back on experience and have confidence in our ability as a crew to carry us through the next few minutes.

The pilot and myself both read through the Rules of Engagement in the cockpit until we are both completely satisfied that we can legally execute the task we have been assigned. The nerves are still present, as there are lots of things that could not go according to plan. The bomb may not guide, the targeting pod could fail; but we suppress the worries, think through how we would deal with such problems should they occur, and get on with the job in hand. The pilot puts the aircraft into the right piece of sky at the correct height, speed and configuration, while I programme and arm the onboard sensors and weapon systems. The final check is made when we receive our weapons clearance. This will only come once friendly assets are clear of the area. Now we can start our attack run.

Trust is the key. We are both busy doing our individual tasks to the best of our ability, whilst at the same time operating as a crew. The pilot must concentrate on flying the aircraft safely and accurately, whilst the weapon systems officer guides the weapon to the target – this is the advantage of a two-man crew.

I call "captured" when the target is centred and is being tracked by our targeting pod. I then read back the laser code with the confirmation of our clearance to drop, and the contact is set. The next thing we hear and feel is a thud as the weapon is released. From 15,000 feet (4,572m) it takes about 33 seconds for the bomb to find its target. During its flight we have to maintain a continuous track, keeping the laser spot on the target to guide the weapon in. Relief floods over us as the weapon hits its designated target. All targeting systems are set to 'safe' mode and we can relax. This whole process may have only taken 3 or 4 minutes, but it feels like hours, culminating in the longest 33 seconds of our lives, until the next time."

Team - *Good communication between pilot and ground crew is vital, in the demanding environment on the flight line.*

Vortices - Low level in the Scottish Highlands, the desolate terrain makes an ideal training ground for the RAF's fast jet crews.

Opposite
Rack - A Tornado GR4 looks most menacing with the wings in full '67 sweep'! This aircraft is shown carrying an impressive weapons load comprising a pair of Storm Shadow missiles on the fuselage pylons, a Sky Shadow Electronic Countermeasure pod on the port outer wing pylon, a BOZ-107 chaff and flare pod on the starboard outer wing pylon and a standard 1,500 litre (330 gallon) fuel tank on the inboard pylon of each wing.

Flash - No. 617 Squadron markings, depicting three red lightning flashes penetrating a dam, are applied to the forward fuselage of squadron aircraft, and worn with pride. The unit is the lead Tornado GR4 squadron for the Storm Shadow missile.

Litening - *Carrying a LITENING III RD targeting pod, this 617 Squadron Tornado GR4 enters the runway prior to departure. The pod provides enhanced target designation for weapon aiming and effectiveness. LITENING III is the latest generation of targeting and navigation pod, which is capable of delivering laser spot detection and tracking, and long-range data and video downlink.*

Ivory *- Tornado GR4 ZA601/AJ-G flaring for touchdown over the 'piano keys' of Runway 05 at Lossiemouth. To commemorate their World War Two predecessors, 617 Squadron has, in recent years, re-adopted the 'AJ' code letter prefix applied to the squadron's Lancaster aircraft for Operation Chastise on May 16, 1943. Operation Chastise was the name of the raid on dams in the German Ruhr valley using the famous bouncing bomb, from which 617 Squadron earned its name - the 'Dambusters'. Tail code 'AJ-G' was first worn by Lancaster BIII (Special) ED932 flown by 617 Squadron's commanding officer, Wing Commander Guy Gibson during the dams raid.*

43(Fighter) Squadron

Gloria Finis - *Glory is the End*

Base: RAF Leuchars, Fife   **Aircraft:** Tornado F3

No. 43(Fighter) Squadron formed at Stirling on 15 April 1916 within the Royal Flying Corps. It moved south in August and went to France in January 1917 for fighter and reconnaissance duties. The squadron returned to the United Kingdom in August 1919 where it disbanded on 31 December. The squadron reformed again at RAF Henlow, Bedfordshire, on 1 July 1925 equipped with Snipes, but replaced these with Gamecocks in 1926 before moving to RAF Tangmere, Kent. Siskins were received in 1928, Furies in 1931 and Hawker Hurricanes arrived in November 1938.

The squadron took part in the Battle of Britain where it was credited with the destruction of 43 enemy aircraft. After the Dieppe raid and the North African invasion, the squadron re-equipped with Spitfires in March 1943 and joined the Desert Air Force to cover the landings in Sicily, Anzio and Salerno. It later covered the landings in Southern France, but returned to Italy in October 1944. After being part of the occupation forces in Austria and Italy the squadron disbanded on 16 May 1947.

The 'Fighting Cocks' reformed at RAF Tangmere with Meteors on 11 February 1949, and moved to RAF Leuchars, Fife, in November 1950. In August 1954, it became the first squadron to fly the Hawker Hunter. It moved to Cyprus in June 1961 and to Aden in March 1963, where it disbanded on 14 October 1967. The squadron reformed again at Leuchars on 1 September 1969 equipped with Phantom FG1s as part of the UK Air Defence Force.

In July 1989 it started to re-equip with Tornado F3s and it deployed to the Gulf in November 1990 as part of the RAF's air defence component, returning after the cessation of hostilities in March 1991. In 1994 it was part of Operation DENY FLIGHT and in December 1999 the squadron deployed to Prince Sultan Air Base, Saudi Arabia, to carry out no-fly zone patrols in Southern Iraq as part of Operation BOLTON. The no-fly zone patrols continued on a four-month rotational basis with the other UK F3 squadrons until Operation TELIC began early in 2003. No.43 Squadron was based in Saudi Arabia for the duration of the conflict, providing air-to-air defensive cover for the coalition strike and support aircraft entering Iraq. The squadron is due to remain in service equipped with Tornado F3s until replaced by Typhoon. In 2005 the Squadron was awarded the Freedom of the City of Stirling in recognition of its origins. When 56(R) Squadron disbanded as the Tornado F3 operational conversion unit in April 2008, 43(F) Squadron absorbed the operational training role and is currently the largest Royal Air Force fighter unit.

Checks - *A junior technician carries out final external checks on this Tornado F3 prior to taxi. This shot features an aircraft undertaking a practice QRA launch to maintain 'Q currency' for the aircrew.*

Defence - 'Golf Foxtrot', fully armed, is launched from Runway 27 at RAF Leuchars during a practice QRA exercise. During the Tornado F3 era, No. 43(F) Squadron's flagship has typically been given the code 'GF' in recognition of the squadron's latin motto – Gloria Finis – meaning 'Glory is the End'.

Freedom - On 4 June 2005, 43(F) Squadron was granted the honour of the Freedom of the City of Stirling, the first Royal Air Force squadron to be granted this honour. The squadron was formed at Falleninch Farm, at the foot of Stirling Castle.

Chequers - *Resplendent in its traditional squadron markings of black and white chequered tail fin and fighter bars astride the nose roundel, and stylised gamecock, the Wing Commanders pennant below the forward canopy identifies 'Golf Foxtrot' as the personal mount of the squadron commander.*

Twilight - *ZE257 was one of the first Tornado F3s delivered to the RAF during the mid 1980s and will see out its remaining flying career at RAF Leuchars. Here the aircraft is being prepared for a night time training sortie on the squadron flight line.*

Blues - *The vivid blue lighting of the weapons systems officer's instrument panels is much in evidence here during night time operations on the 43 Squadron ramp.*

Flight Lieutenant Roy Macintyre is a Tornado F3 instructor pilot with over 4000 flying hours on type. He describes what it is like for a student on their first flight at night.

"On paper not much changes at night. The atmosphere provides the same lift to the wings. It's just that your eyes can't show you where you are going as well. Actually, there are a number of subtle traps awaiting the student on their first night sortie. The first occurs in the planning phase – don't make notes or mark maps in the same colour as the blue or red cockpit lights as they will become invisible once airborne! After strapping in, getting the illumination levels right takes a bit of time; there are over fifteen separate light dimmers in the front cockpit alone.

For a student pilot just getting to the runway is a new challenge. The myriad of airfield lights changes the familiar daytime scene into a complicated pattern of blue, red, green and white. Lined up, ready to go, another problem awaits the inexperienced. The RAF does not practice 'pairs' takeoffs at night, the second jet rolls 20 or 30 seconds after the first, the temptation to look at the beautiful blue-white afterburner flames of the lead fighter as it roars away is overwhelming. However your night vision is destroyed instantly. The more experienced pilots shut their eyes until the lead fighter is well into the distance."

cont'd page 76

Intense - *Until one witnesses a night time Tornado F3 launch at close quarters it is difficult to appreciate the magnitude and beauty of the white hot afterburner flames from the two Turbo Union RB199 turbofan engines.*

Bubble - *An unusual close-up view of the Tornado F3s front canopy.*

cont'd from page 75

"Night exercises practiced during the operational conversion unit course, while basic compared to the front line (no instruction is given on the use of night-vision goggles), still provide demanding tests for the students, particularly to pilots. Ensuring two aircraft remain safely separated at all times while manoeuvring into the required positions takes a great deal of concentration. For the weapon systems officer, bringing the fighter to within 750ft (250m) of a completely unlit aircraft is a task that still challenges the most skilled of squadron aircrew.

We usually save the best until last - night-time air-to-air refuelling. Some love it, some hate it. Either way, it pushes crew co-operation to the limit to get the job done and fuel into the tanks. Unlike many other aspects of military flying, it doesn't seem to get easier with practice but is a vital skill for modern air defence, as Operation TELIC showed."

Pushback - *Until recently, the Northern HAS (Hardened Aircraft Shelter) complex at RAF Leuchars was home to the 'Fighting Cocks'. Tasked with the Tornado F3 training role, the squadron now operates from the fighter station's main ramp - the former home of 56(R) Squadron. HAS operations differ somewhat to those on a flightline, the necessity to push back the aircraft into the shelter after recovery being just one event.*

Jetwash - On a bright, crisp winter's day at RAF Leuchars, this Tornado F3 appears to be surfing on a sea of jellied-air created by its playmate lifting off just out of shot.

Pristine - The pilot of 'Golf Hotel' deploys the thrust reverser buckets during the landing sequence at RAF Leuchars. Despite the clean appearance of the aircraft's tail in this photo, the use of the thrust reverser buckets means the tail will not stay clean for long.

Track - *A 43(F) Squadron Tornado F3 holds station with a VC-10 C1K tanker after completing a leg of a 'racetrack' pattern flown within a designated air-refuelling area off the East Coast of Scotland.*

Migrate - Callsign *'Gamecock 1'* rolls down the Leuchars runway for an afternoon sortie in early winter. Darkness comes early in Scotland during the depths of winter giving only six to seven hours of daylight.

111(Fighter) Squadron

Adstantes - *Standing by (them)*

Base: RAF Leuchars, Fife   **Aircraft:** Tornado F3

No. 111(Fighter) Squadron formed at Deir-el-Belah, Palestine on 1 August 1917 as a fighter squadron. Flying a variety of aircraft, the squadron supported the British Army against the Turks in Palestine and Syria. In October 1918 it moved to Egypt, and disbanded on 1 February 1920. On 1 October 1923, 111 Squadron reformed at Duxford, Cambridgeshire, as a fighter squadron, equipped with Grebes. Snipes were added the following year and it subsequently flew Siskins, Bulldogs and Gauntlets.

In January 1938, 111 squadron was chosen as the RAF's first Hurricane squadron and flew the type on defensive duties at the beginning of World War Two. The squadron later took part in the Battle of Britain, where it was credited with 65 victories. Spitfires were received in April 1941, which were used for offensive sweeps over France and bomber-escort duties. In November 1942, the Squadron moved to Gibraltar and, thereafter, supported the 1st Army in Algeria and Tunisia before moving to Malta in June 1943 to cover the invasion of Sicily. It was later based in Italy and Corsica but disbanded at Treviso on 12 May 1947.

The squadron reformed at North Weald, Essex, on 2 December 1953, equipped with Meteor F8s. These were replaced with Hunters in June 1955 with which the squadron achieved international fame with its 'Black Arrows' aerobatic team, flying a 22 aircraft loop. No. 111(F) Squadron moved to RAF Wattisham, Suffolk, in June 1958 where it converted to the Lightning F1A in April 1961. Upgrading to the F3 in December 1964, it flew this type until September 1974. It re-equipped with Phantom FGR2s at RAF Coningsby, Lincolnshire, on 1 October 1974 and moved to RAF Leuchars, Fife, on 3 November 1975. In 1978, the squadron began conversion to the Phantom FG1 following the type's retirement from the Fleet Air Arm.

The last Phantom sortie was flown on 30 January 1990 and, after re-equipping with the Tornado F3, 'Treble-One' was declared operational again on 31 December 1990. No. 111(F) Squadron was involved in Operation DENY FLIGHT over Bosnia in the mid-1990s and began a policing role over the Southern Iraqi no-fly zones in 1999 as part of Operation BOLTON, later Operation RESINATE, the UK element of Operation SOUTHERN WATCH. The squadron deployed to the Gulf again in February 2003 as part of Operation TELIC, the UK contingent of Operation IRAQI FREEDOM. The 'Treble-One' led detachment was flying 16 combat air patrols a day in support of the ground and air campaign. The squadron continues its commitment to man the Northern Quick Reaction Alert (QRA) and the Falkland Islands, in addition to participating in large multi-national air exercises around the world.

Split - *In 2007, the squadron celebrated its 90th Anniversary. As part of the celebrations, a Hurricane MkI rendezvoused with 111(F) Squadron's specially painted Tornado F3.*

Icon *- Almost 70 years of history separate these two iconic fighter aircraft. Note the high angle of attack maintained by the Tornado F3 in order to hold station with its World War Two counterpart. This Hurricane MkI is a genuine Battle of Britain survivor, which was found in a derelict condition in a university campus in India. The aircraft's owner Peter Vacher restored the aircraft, which actually flew with 111(F) Squadron during World War Two.*

Mirror - *Weapon Systems Officer's view of the Tornado F3 rear cockpit, seen through the helmet visor!*

1917
2007
ZE734
FLT LT J DUNN
SQN LDR D J HUNT
O BANDEIRANTE 3
RESCUE

Swept - Banking away from the camera-ship, 'Juliet Uniform' carries a single dummy ASRAAM on the port wing pylon. The two recesses in the aircraft's underbelly are used to carry AMRAAM missiles. A 'RAIDS' pod (Rangeless Airborne Instrumented Debriefing System) is carried under the starboard wing. This pod records the exact position of the aircraft during the flight and this data can later be played back on a computer. This is extremely worthwhile during a large scale exercise as the whole mission of all aircraft involved can be replayed and analysed.

Opposite

Tremblers - It's not every RAF squadron which can claim to own one specially painted aircraft, let alone two! In 2007, 111(F) Squadron had the distinction of operating two such aircraft. Tornado F3 ZG753/HH, the aircraft closest to the camera, bore the unusual inscription 'O Bandeirante 3'. The name 'O Bandeirante' was first carried by 111(F) Squadron Spitfire Vb BM634 during 1942, in honour of the British citizens and Brazilian nationals living in Brazil who raised money to buy Spitfires for the RAF during World War Two. The aircraft crashed shortly after it was delivered, but a second 111(F) Squadron Spitfire Vb, EP166, later carried the name. To commemorate this, 'Hotel Hotel' became the third aircraft to carry the name 'O Bandeirante'.

History - Tornado F3 ZE734/JU flies over the UK's most famous hill figure – the White Horse at Uffington in Oxfordshire. The non-standard tail code worn by ZE734 was applied to represent the wartime code letters used by No. 111(F) Squadron during World War Two, originally worn by Hurricanes and then by Spitfires from 1941 onwards.

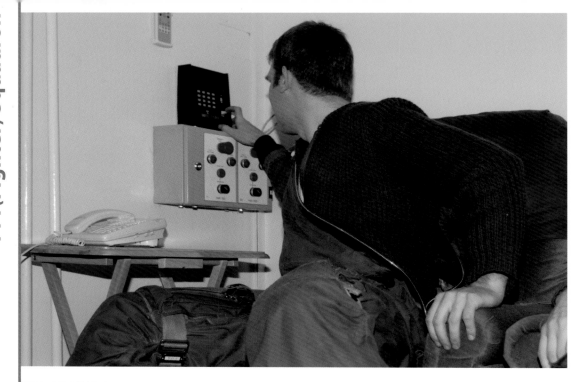

Tornado F3 pilot Flight Lieutenant Richard Pargeter shares the experience of intercepting a Russian bomber during a Quick Reaction Alert (QRA) mission.

"Dan's leg restraints clang as he walks down the corridor to wake us up again. I look at my watch and it is 3.30am. Tonight has turned from excitement to tedium; two Tu-95 Bear aircraft had been detected on the radar off the North coast of Norway and were now somewhere else over the North Atlantic trying to hide below radar cover. We've been up almost all night on false alarms that the Russian bombers were coming towards the UK, but still no contact. And now we're up again, fully dressed in our goon bags (submersion suits). I make everyone in the QRA crew room a cup of tea and sit in one of the armchairs exhausted. Sitting, I realise I'm as happy as I've ever been. I'm the junior pilot on 111(F) Squadron; this is my second time on Q; and here I am, just like all the fighter pilots of years gone by, tired and sat in an armchair, waiting. Things are turning back to excitement though as the secure communications link scratches into life, we silently listen….SCRAMBLE!

Within minutes I'm airborne and heading to a CAP (combat air patrol) over the Western Isles of Scotland to show our presence, two Tornado F3s – fully 'tooled-up'. We wait, we tank in the dark, then we wait again on CAP. I notice a fuel asymmetry problem and we think we might have to return to base but it's okay, problem sorted, we're back on track. On my second tanking, this time just as day breaks, the ground controller seems to be getting irate. With our radar off during the tanking we are blind and are trying to build a mental picture. They're close and as soon as I unplug I get tally-ho even before the radar gets them, seven miles north; a pair of them, one above the other. OK, we've now got nine tonnes of gas to use so I put in the burners and start the chase. My Weapon Systems Officer is giving an excellent service but somehow I still over-cook the join and have to 'wash-off' a lot of speed, and at 28,000ft (8,534m) there is not much air to slow you down. I have to use airbrake, manoeuvre flaps, but somehow I just stop solidly on the trail-man's wing – perfect – it didn't surprise him, but it definitely surprised me!

This is it then, my five years training has peaked at this, defending the integrity of the UK's airspace – but it's not quite worth all the hype, this is not a shooting war with dogfights - the worst case scenario that my training has geared me up for. This is flying on the wing of a non-hostile aircraft, reporting its disposition back to ground control. I feel that anyone could do this – but I wouldn't change it for anything. We wave to the Russian aircrew and they wave back – I'm sure they feel the same, glad to be in the company of other aviators somewhere over the North Atlantic. There is a common bond and I'd like to buy the crew a beer for this opportunity to do my job."

Opposite (top)
Scramble! - The pilot of Q1 (the designator of one of two Tornado F3s on QRA) receives a message from the scrambler phone in the crew room within the purpose-built Quick Reaction Alert (QRA) facility at RAF Leuchars. This brief message will trigger the start of 10 minutes of frenetic activity, which will culminate in the launch of QRA North's primary alert aircraft.

Opposite (bottom)
Sprint - After receiving the initial message to scramble, the crew of Q1 sprint to the fully armed Tornado F3 situated in a Hardened Aircraft Shelter (HAS) located near to the QRA facility.

Ready - No.111(F) Squadron is now one of two Tornado F3 units tasked to provide crews and aircraft at 10 minutes readiness, 365 days a year, to police the UK's airspace. The 2,250 litre (495 gallon) drop-tanks under each wing are carried by Tornado F3s as standard for QRA.

Potent - *Aircraft on QRA operations typically carry four AIM-120 Advanced Medium-Range Air-to-Air Missiles (AMRAAMs) and four Advanced Short-Range Air-to-Air Missiles (ASRAAM). The Tornado F3 also carries live high-explosive rounds for its internally mounted 27mm Mauser cannon.*

120 Squadron

Endurance

Base: RAF Kinloss, Moray   **Aircraft:** Nimrod MR2

No. 120 Squadron formed at Cramlington in Northumberland on 1 January 1918 during World War One and was equipped with DH 9 aircraft. It was intended that the squadron should join in the bombing of Germany but the Armistice was signed before the squadron became operational and its role changed to mail carrying between Hawkinge, Kent and France. In May 1919 it re-equipped with DH 10s and earned considerable publicity by flying non-stop from Hawkinge to Cologne, Germany in the then unheard-of time of three hours. However, with the post-war contraction of the RAF, the squadron disbanded on 28 August 1919.

No. 120 Squadron reformed in World War Two on 2 June 1941 and was tasked with protecting trans-Atlantic convoys. Equipped with long-range Liberator aircraft, it flew anti U-boat and convoy protection patrols initially from Northern Ireland and, between April 1943 and March 1944, from Reykjavik in Iceland. During World War Two, 120 Squadron was the Royal Air Force's top-scoring anti-submarine unit, being credited with the destruction of twelve U-boats, three others shared and at least a further eight damaged.

After a short disbandment 120 Squadron reformed in October 1946 and in the ensuing years saw service in Palestine (now Israel), Canada, Australia, the Far East, the Caribbean and Norway, flying Lancaster GR3s and ASR3s and Shackleton MR1s, MR2s and MR3s. From December 1970 onwards Nimrods replaced the Shackletons and since then the squadron has flown world-wide in anti-submarine, surface surveillance and Search and Rescue operations.

In January 1977 the new task of patrolling the UK's 200-mile (320km) fishing limit commenced. The squadron re-equipped with the improved Nimrod MR2 version in 1981. As a result of the Argentine seizure of the Falkland Islands in April 1982, 120 Squadron soon became involved in Operation CORPORATE to liberate the islands. Its aircraft operated from Ascension Island and were progressively fitted with Sidewinder air-to-air and Harpoon air-to-surface missiles. In October 1983 Her Majesty Queen Elizabeth II awarded the squadron the battle honour 'South Atlantic 1982'. In 1991 crews from 120 Squadron deployed to Oman as part of the Allied Gulf War forces and surveillance and anti-shipping patrols were flown in the Persian Gulf. The squadron also sent crews to the Adriatic in support of United Nations sanctions against the former Yugoslavia. In more recent times 120 Squadron has deployed crews to various airfields in the Middle East to support coalition forces in the Iraq War and the continuing War Against Terrorism.

Servicing - Depth maintenance of the Nimrod MR2 fleet is carried out by BAe Systems under the Nimrod Integrated Support Contract at RAF Kinloss.

Page 91

Hunter - Developed to counteract the increasing threat from Soviet submarines, the Nimrod was developed by Hawker Siddeley in the mid-1960s. Based on the Comet Mk4C airframe, the Nimrod MR1 entered service in 1969, replacing the RAF's fleet of elderly maritime reconnaissance Avro Shackletons. Upgraded to MR2 standard during the late 1970s and early 1980s, today this versatile platform continues to play a vital role in the RAF's Intelligence Surveillance Target Acquisition and Reconnaissance (ISTAR) capability. RAF Kinloss is home to two front line units – 120 and 201 Squadrons and an Operational Conversion Unit – 42(R) Squadron, operating a pooled fleet of fifteen aircraft. The Nimrod MR2 is still the world's only jet-powered maritime patrol aircraft in military service.

Line - Day-to-day servicing and first line maintenance of the Nimrod MR2 fleet is carried out by the Nimrod Line Squadron.

Role - *Both front line squadrons carry out identical roles that include routine training sorties, Search And Rescue missions, Anti-Submarine Warfare, Anti-Surface Warfare and on operational deployment in the Middle East in support of coalition troops in Afghanistan or Iraq.*

Boom - *Distinctive to the Nimrod MR2 is rear tail boom housing the Magnetic Anomaly Detector (MAD). The device can recognise disturbances in the Earth's magnetic field caused by submarines below the ocean surface. XV226, shown here, was the first production Nimrod MR1 which first flew in June 1968, and was used extensively on the Nimrod development programme. This example finally entered RAF service in early 1973.*

Dome - *Both sides of the forward fuselage include an inward-opening bubble-type observation window used by observers to photograph suspected targets clearly.*

201 Squadron

Hic et ubique - *Here and everywhere*

Base: RAF Kinloss, Moray   **Aircraft:** Nimrod MR2

Standby - One of the main roles undertaken by the Nimrod MR2 force is Search And Rescue (SAR). One aircraft remains on constant standby at RAF Kinloss. During a live SAR operation, the Nimrod is used as the on-scene command and control hub. Its crew uses HF, VHF and UHF radios to establish communication with the vessel in distress. Information is relayed between the vessel, the land-based Aeronautical Rescue Coordination Centre (ARCC) and the en-route SAR helicopter. This provides the crew of the SAR helicopter with information about the state of the vessel and casualties onboard in advance of arriving on the scene. During larger incidents, where there could be several helicopters involved in the SAR operation, the Nimrod will take on the role of Air Asset Command, organising search sectors for all the rescue helicopters on scene.

No. 201 Squadron was formed as 1 Squadron of the Royal Naval Air Service on 16 October 1914. During the early part of World War One the squadron took part in the first ever engagement against a submarine and later flew fighter patrols over the Western Front. On 1 April 1918 it was absorbed into the newly formed RAF and renumbered 201 Squadron. It returned to the United Kingdom and disbanded on 31 December. The squadron reformed at Calshot, Hampshire, on 1 January 1929 with Supermarine Southamptons.

An affiliation with Guernsey was announced in 1939 and led to the first of many visits to the island. During World War Two, flying Shorts Sunderlands, 201 Squadron attacked some 20 enemy submarines, sinking seven, and was awarded one DSO, 12 DFCs and 11 DFMs. The squadron played a vital part in the Berlin Airlift in 1948 before disbanding at Pembroke Dock on 28 February 1957. No. 201 Squadron reformed at RAF St Mawgan, Cornwall on 1 October 1958 after the renumbering of 220 Squadron, and resumed its worldwide maritime duties flying Avro Shackletons MR3s. It moved to Kinloss, Moray on 14 March 1965.

In October 1970 the squadron was the first to receive Nimrod MR1s providing it with the world's first jet maritime patrol aircraft. These have since been upgraded to MR2 standard and were involved in the Falklands campaign in 1982. In August 1990, 201 Squadron was involved in the first deployment to Seeb, Oman, for the Gulf conflict with Iraq, first enforcing UN sanctions and then flying surface surveillance missions. Between 1993 and 1995 the squadron deployed regularly to NAS Sigonella in Sicily where it supported UN resolutions enforcing the maritime blockade of the former Yugoslavian Republic.

After the terrorist events of 11 September 2001 the squadron returned to Seeb, expanding its operating environment to the overland theatre in support of ground forces, as well as its more traditional anti-submarine warfare role in the Gulf of Oman. In February 2003, 201 Squadron continued to provide support for naval forces in the Arabian Gulf during the second Gulf conflict; with the introduction of a new optical sensor, adding tasking including the search for Weapons of Mass Destruction and the support of ground forces in Iraq.

The special relationship with Guernsey continues to this day and culminated in the squadron being granted the Privilege of the Island in 1994. With ever-present strategic uncertainties, the squadron remains ready to respond to the challenges to world peace and security.

Drop - *The Nimrod on SAR standby is also capable of dropping Air Sea Rescue (ASR) life rafts and survival packs stored in the bomb bay.*

Smokin' *- Nimrod MR2 XV260 touches down after a six-hour training sortie over the North Sea. A typical sortie can involve several tasks such as a surface search – photographing fishing boats or other vessels, a simulated submarine detection exercise and a Search And Rescue exercise.*

Clutch *- Air Traffic Control is just one agency vital to the day-to-day running of an RAF station. Due to the close proximity of Kinloss and Lossiemouth (known as Clutch Airfields), the latter provides radar coverage for both stations. Here, a controller in the Kinloss visual tower gives taxi clearance to a Nimrod on the flight line.*

Camouflage - *This shot of Nimrod MR2 XV231 shows to good effect the new all-over 'camouflage grey', which is gradually replacing the previous hemp colour scheme.*

Crew - The twelve-strong Nimrod MR2 crew comprises a pilot, co-pilot and flight engineer on the flight deck, three weapon systems officers (WSOs) – one tactical, one routine, and one who is the sensor and communications co-ordinator. The co-ordinator is supported by six weapon systems operators (WSOps) dubbed 'wet' (two) and 'dry' (four). Wet crewmembers deal with everything below the water surface utilising the aircraft's acoustic sensors, which monitor the sonobuoys. Dry crewmembers deal with activities above the water surface, utilising the aircraft's radios, radar and electronic support measures (ESM) equipment.

Search And Rescue

202 Squadron, D Flight

Semper vigilate - *Be always vigilant*

Base: RAF Lossiemouth, Moray **Aircraft:** Sea King HAR3

No. 202 Squadron's origins extend back to 2 Squadron, Royal Naval Air Service (RNAS), which formed at Eastchurch, Kent, on 17 October 1914. Equipped with a variety of aircraft it moved to Dover, Kent, in February 1915 but lost its number plate in June that year, when it became 2 Wing. It reformed again at Dunkirk, Belgium, during November 1916, and was renumbered 202 Squadron on 1 April 1918. It returned to the United Kingdom in March 1919 and disbanded on 22 January 1920. The squadron reformed at Alexandria, Egypt, on 9 April 1920 as a naval co-operation unit, disbanding on 16 May 1921.

No. 202 Squadron reformed on 1 January 1929 at Kalafrana in Malta, equipped with Fairey IIID seaplanes, which were replaced with Fairey IIIFs in 1930. Supermarine Scapas, the squadron's first flying boats, were received in May 1935 and these were replaced in September 1937 with Saro Londons, which were flown on anti-submarine patrols. A move to Alexandria was made in September 1938, but at the outbreak of World War Two, the squadron moved to Gibraltar to patrol the approaches to the Mediterranean. In September 1940 Swordfish float-planes were added for local patrol duties, but 1941 saw the arrival of Catalina and Sunderland flying boats.

The squadron moved to Northern Ireland in September 1944 to conduct U-boat patrols off the West coast, disbanding on 12 June 1945. No. 202 Squadron reformed at RAF Aldergrove, Northern Ireland, on 1 October 1946 equipped with Halifaxes for meteorological flights over the Atlantic. Hastings were received in October 1950 and flown until the squadron disbanded on 31 July 1964. On 1 September 1964, 228 Squadron, a Search and Rescue unit, was renumbered 202 Squadron. SAR flights were operated from RAF Coltishall, Norfolk, RAF Acklington, Northumberland, and RAF Leuchars, Fife, as well as at the HQ at RAF Leconfield, Yorkshire.

In 1978 and 1979, Whirlwinds were replaced by Sea King HAR3s with 'A' Flight at RAF Boulmer, Northumberland, 'B' Flight at RAF Brawdy, Pembrokeshire, 'C' Flight at RAF Coltishall, Norfolk, and 'D' Flight at RAF Lossiemouth, Moray. In 1988 its headquarters moved to Boulmer and 'E' Flight was later formed at Leconfield. In another re-organisation in July 1994, 'B' and 'C' Flights went to 22 Squadron, leaving 202 Squadron with 'A', 'D' and 'E' Flights.

Vigilant - *Other than the The Red Arrows, the bright yellow Search And Rescue (SAR) Sea King HAR3s are probably the most publicly recognisable RAF asset today. Operated by 22, 202 and 203(R) Squadrons, the Sea Kings are based at strategic locations throughout the UK. RAF Lossiemouth is home to 202 Squadron's D Flight, equipped with two Sea Kings, one of which is maintained at a constant state of readiness, 24 hours a day, 365 days a year.*

Drill - *The primary role of SAR Sea Kings is the recovery of downed military aviators. Periodically, aircrew must undergo sea drills in order to simulate an ejection over water and subsequent rescue. After being dropped overboard from a specially equipped vessel, the survivor is kept afloat by a life saving jacket. Prior to rescue, the survivor must haul in the attached survival pack, inflate the life raft and await rescue by the Sea King.*

Survival - *The back end crew of an RAF SAR Sea King normally comprises a winch man (a trained paramedic) and a winch operator. This shot shows the victim being winched up to the cabin by the Sea King's hydraulic winch in a double strop. A horizontal or sitting attitude is considered much safer for survivors suffering from the effects of cold-water immersion.*

Exercise - *D Flight regularly exercises with Royal National Lifeboat Institution lifeboats up and down the North and East coasts of Scotland. The crew of 'Inchcape', Arbroath's lifeboat, enjoys some valuable winch training off the coast of Angus.*

Foam - Due to their busy workload, the Sea Kings' familiar high-visibility paint doesn't remain clean for very long. Cleaning off the sooty deposits created by the Sea King's two Rolls-Royce Gnome engines is no easy task!

Readiness - Between 08:00 and 22:00 hours each day, one Sea King will be at a 15-minute readiness state during the crew's 24-hour shift. Outside of these hours the readiness state is reduced to 45 minutes. Overnight, crew stay in purpose-built accommodation in D Flight's building.

Search and Rescue services

Aeronautical Rescue Coordination Centre & Mountain Rescue Teams

Base: RAF Kinloss, Moray (ARCC & MRT), RAF Leuchars, Fife (MRT)

Information - *The primary role of the Aeronautical Rescue Coordination Centre (ARCC) is to assist in the recovery of downed military aircrew through the efficient coordination of information and assets. In peacetime however, the majority of rescues involve civilians. The RAF Search and Rescue Organisation was set-up in 1941, and was tasked with assisting military aircrew in distress over land or sea. To enable the effective coordination of this new organisation, two centres were opened at Plymouth and Pitreavie. The ARCC was opened in 1996 following the closure of Pitreavie Castle. The centre took on the responsibility for the whole of the UK by the end of 1997, providing approximately one million square miles of cover. It is equipped with a purpose-designed Rescue Coordination System (RCS) which gives controllers instant access to a vast database of assets and emergency services, and allows detailed logging of incidents in real time. The system can provide instant communications to all military SAR units, RAF Mountain Rescue Teams (MRT) as well as numerous Coastguard, Police and local authority centres.*

Assets - *The ARCC is staffed by approximately 40 personnel working shift patterns. Day-to-day, the staff on duty will comprise an operations control officer assisted by a senior non-commissioned officer plus a second assistant. Additional staff may be called in as and when required should an incident arise. The ARCC can call on a range of air assets at 15 minutes readiness including Royal Air Force and Royal Navy Sea Kings and Coastguard S-61 and S-92 helicopters stationed the length and breadth of the UK, plus a Nimrod MR2 on permanent 2 hour standby at RAF Kinloss. Whilst many rescues owe their success to the technology, ARCC staff often have to rely on nebulous pieces of information from those directly involved in an incident, meaning that common sense and experience are equally as important as modern technology. The ARCC is also home to the UK Mission Control Centre (UKMCC), which utilises low earth-orbiting and geostationary satellites to detect emergency distress beacons across the globe. The UKMCC is part of a wider organisation which uses COSPAS-SARSAT satellite-aided tracking system to detect and locate those in distress. The UKMCC then processes the distress signal and initiates an alert to the appropriate search and rescue authorities.*

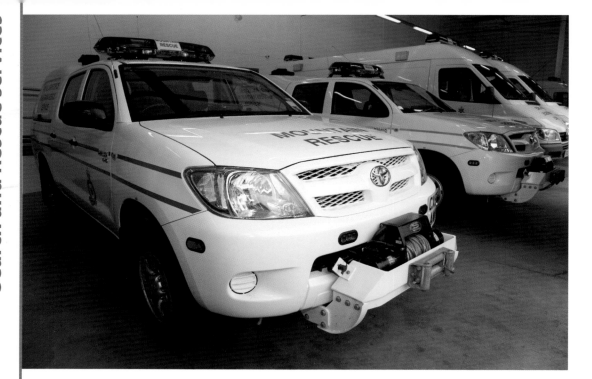

Fleet - RAF Mountain Rescue Teams (MRT) are an integral part of the UKSAR organisation, who work closely with SAR helicopters and civilian mountain rescue teams. All teams have a modern fleet of well-equipped emergency response vehicles.

Whensoever - Although RAF MRTs were established originally to assist pilots and passengers of aircraft that had crashed or force-landed in the mountainous regions of the UK, most callouts today are to injured or missing hill climbers. Both Scottish-based MRTs at Kinloss and Leuchars have 7 or 8 full-time staff as well as around 30 part-time volunteers. The team as a whole will deploy on exercise every weekend, whilst individual members are expected to attend a minimum of two weekends in each month, as well as being available for callouts day or night. Exercises usually consist of walking and climbing, with various rescue techniques and medical training being practiced.

Cab - *The crew of the Sea King HU5 normally comprises pilot and co-pilot, plus observer and aircrewman in the back. Each member of the back seat crew is able to administer immediate emergency care, the aircrewman normally having advanced medical training.*

Opposite

Exercise - *The team, in this case RAF Leuchars MRT, will also regularly exercise in the mountains with the SAR Sea Kings from RAF Lossiemouth or, as seen here, from HMS Gannet at Prestwick, providing both MRT personnel and helicopter crew with valuable training experience.*

Gannet - *In addition to the RAF's yellow Sea King HAR3s, a large part of Scotland's SAR coverage is actually provided by the Royal Navy's red and grey Sea King HU5s of HMS Gannet SAR Flight, based at Prestwick International Airport. The flight has a huge area of responsibility, from Ben Nevis in the north to the Isle of Man in the south, Edinburgh in the east and to Northern Ireland and beyond in the west. Depending on the geographical area of the tasking, the RAF and Royal Navy will often work together during these operations. Here, an HMS Gannet Sea King is about to pick up RAF Leuchars MRT in Glen Coe for a joint exercise.*

Flying Experience

661 Volunteer Gliding Squadron

Base: Kirknewton, West Lothian   **Aircraft:** Viking T1

Compact - *A typical early Saturday morning for the instructors and staff of 661 Volunteer Gliding Squadron involves carefully decanting the squadron's fleet of six Grob 103 Viking T1s from their hangar using swivel trolleys.*

Originally formed at Strathaven, in South Lanarkshire when air cadet gliding was formally established in 1942, 1 Gliding School (GS), as it was then known, moved a few miles south to Dungavel, South Lanaskshire in April 1944. By 1950 the school had moved again to Dumfries, Dumfries and Galloway. Initially the GSs were part of the RAF's Reserve Command but in 1955, Flying Training Command took over the responsibility and they became known as Volunteer Gliding Schools (VGSs).

At that time the school was on the move again, this time back to the East coast to RAF Turnhouse, on the outskirts of Edinburgh, where it became known as 661 VGS. The school was to enjoy nine years operating from the capital until it was made homeless in 1964. For three years the volunteer staff would travel all the way up to the then HMS (now RM) Condor near Arbroath, Angus, to retain their currency.

The school officially re-opened on the 2nd April 1967 at its current home - the former RAF aerodrome at Kirknewton - after the US Air Force had vacated the site the previous year. At the time, 661 VGS operated a fleet of gliders comprising two Slingsby T21 Sedbergh TX1s, four Slingsby T31 Cadet TX3s and a Swallow TX1, which was one of three gifted to the Air Training Corps by the MacRobert's Trust.

After 35 years of service with 661 VGS, the Cadet TX3s and Sedberghs were retired in 1988 and replaced by Grob G103 Viking T1s. The unit is currently equipped with six Viking T1s and is manned by a staff of around thirty volunteers, led by Squadron Leader Allan Gillespie RAFVR(T). Squadron Leader Gillespie joined 661 VGS as a staff cadet at Turnhouse in 1967, climbing the ranks to become commanding officer in 1998. In 2005, all Volunteer Gliding Schools underwent a subtle name change and became Volunteer Gliding Squadrons as part of changes to the command structure.

Preparation - *The gliders are launched using up to six flexible steel cables stored in drums in a winch tractor located at the opposite end from the launch point.*

Launch - *The cable is initially reeled in slowly after the call is given to 'Take up slack'. Once the launch cable is taut, the 'All out' signal is given and the winch driver at the opposite end of the runway applies the power to launch the glider.*

Climb - *Winch-launched gliders experience an incredible rate of climb in the first few seconds of flight. Note the red parachute used to steady the cable once released by the pilot. Once it has fallen to earth, the cable is reeled in by the winch in preparation for the next series of launches.*

Touchdown - The Vikings at Kirknewton generally use a tarmac strip for launch, while recoveries take place on both grass and tarmac. Here the moment of touchdown is captured. The air brake on the upper surface of the port wing can be clearly seen in the raised position, whilst wheel brakes are utilised once on the runway.

Ready - The squadron's fleet of Vikings are lined up ready to commence the morning's flying programme.

Opposite (middle)
Beginnings - The Gliding Induction Course (GIC) teaches the basic principals of flying. During a cadet's first visit to a Viking-equipped VGS, he or she will be taught the GIC1 which comprises three launches. Subsequent visits will see the cadet progress onto the GIC2 (four launches) and GIC3 (five launches). On completion of the course the cadet will be awarded a GIC certificate.

Briefing - Staff and cadets gather outside the launch point caravan for a briefing prior to the first launch of the day. The winch driver receives his instructions to launch using a series of flashing light signals from the caravan.

Above

Flex - The Viking T1 is dual control, with the cadet normally taking up the front seat position and the instructor in the rear. With a wingspan of 17.5m (57ft), the flex on the wings is much in evidence here.

Expectation - A group of excited Air Cadets wait their turn for the next available seat. No. 661 VGS has a large catchment area, which includes much of south and central Scotland, Edinburgh and Glasgow. Launches at Kirknewton can be quite prolific given the right conditions. For many of these youngsters, this will be their first experience of flying.

Downwind - *The entire fleet of Air Cadet gliders wear unique and distinctive two digit codes on the tail and the underside of the wings, which improves identification between pilots in the air. Orange day glo stripes are also worn on the wings to improve visibility. Here 'Victor Victor' is captured in the downwind leg prior to recovery.*

662 Volunteer Gliding Squadron

Sapientus Icaro - *Wiser than Icarus*

Base: RM Condor, Angus   **Aircraft:** Viking T1

Over 200 Gliding Schools were formed during World War Two, those numbered 1 to 10 being based in Scotland. The roots of 662 VGS can be found within two of these original gliding schools.

No. 2 Gliding School (GS) formed in October of 1942 at East Fortune, East Lothian but was disbanded shortly after the end of the war. It reformed at the end of 1947 at Grangemouth, Stirlingshire and in 1955 after a move to Edzell, Angus, it became known as 662 Volunteer Gliding School (VGS) when the Gliding Squadrons became part of Flying Training Command.

No. 5 Gliding School was formed towards the end of the war at Fordoun, Kincardineshire and subsequently relocated to Dyce, Aberdeenshire in May 1946. It was later absorbed into 662 VGS in 1955 with a detached flight at Dyce. This detached flight was later to become 663 VGS. In 1958, 662 VGS moved to its present home at the then HMS (now RM) Condor, on the outskirts of Arbroath, Angus.

Initially flying the Slingsby Cadet TX3 and Slingsby Sedbergh TX1, the school also operated a single Slingsby Prefect TX1 from 1958. In 1963, the school was presented with a Slingsby Swallow TX1, plus a trailer, by the MacRobert's Trust and was the first of its type to be operated by the Air Training Corps. This aircraft provided the school with over 20 years of service before finally being withdrawn from use in 1984. Under the command of Squadron Leader Lovat Fraser, the unit re-equipped with the new two-seat Grob Viking T1. Following a change in command structure in 2005, 662 VGS became a Volunteer Gliding Squadron. Currently commanded by Squadron Leader Bob Lyle, RAFVR(T), the squadron operates a fleet of eight Grob Viking T1 two-seat gliders from the Royal Marines base.

Countless numbers of cadets who achieved their first solo in gliders with 662 VGS became military or commercial airline pilots. Three former 662 VGS cadets became Red Arrows pilots and one became a Concorde pilot.

Reflection - *Gliding is very much dependent on the weather, and after an early morning assessment of the prevailing wind and cloud base, the staff and cadets of 662 VGS will drive from their headquarters building to the other side of the airfield to begin the process of extracting the gliders from the hangar. The winch and launch control caravan are towed to opposite ends of the active runway. Depending on the intensity of the day's flying programme, a number of the squadron's Viking T1s will then be towed to the caravan and prepared for the first launch.*

Tower - Flying from an airfield that was once a very active Royal Naval Air Station, the Viking T1 gliders of 662 VGS are now the only aircraft which can regularly be seen in the skies above RM Condor. Now home to 45 Commando, Royal Marines, much of the infrastructure of the Royal Navy's air engineer school still remains. The squadron's headquarters are situated in the old control tower, which now houses its briefing rooms, offices and classrooms.

Opposite:
Airborne - The Air Cadet Organisation (ACO) operates some 83 Viking T1s, shared between 11 Volunteer Gliding Squadrons around the UK. The Air Cadet Central Gliding School (ACCGS) at Syerston, Nottinghamshire, also uses the type to train the VGS instructors. No. 662 VGS currently operate eight of the Grob-built glider, making it one of the largest squadrons in the UK. This particular example, 'Yankee Sierra', has launched well over 15,000 times since it was delivered to the ACO - an indication of the volume of work carried out by the Volunteer Gliding Squadrons.

Lift - The Viking T1 is seen by many as the first stepping-stone to a career in the Royal Air Force. Those air cadets with the right level of motivation and ability may rise to the challenge and go 'above and beyond'.

Originally formed at Abbotsinch Airport, now Glasgow International, 663 VGS came into being in July 1967 at Dyce Airport, Aberdeen, where they flew a single Slingsby Sedbergh TX1 and a Slingsby Kirby Cadet TX3. The following year saw another move to Inverness Airport at Dalcross. However, the considerable commuting distance for many of the instructors meant a return to Dyce just a few months later in November of 1968.

The unit saw almost five years of operations at Dyce Airport, but the flourishing oil industry meant that the airport was becoming increasingly busy, and after various successful summer continuation courses at RAF Milltown, Moray, the commander at that time, Squadron Leader Sandy Reid, applied to relocate the school to this station. Permission was granted, and in the summer of 1973 the school moved to this World War Two satellite airfield located three miles from Lossiemouth. From here, 663 VGS trained many cadets, including HRH Prince Andrew whilst a pupil at the nearby Gordonstoun School. Less than four years later however, 663 VGS was again on the move, this time to its current home at RAF Kinloss, Moray. The Royal links continued here when HRH Prince Edward followed in his brother's footsteps and attended the school for his Air Experience Flying in 1980.

A big step for 663 VGS came in 1986 when the unit took delivery of a pair of Slingsby-built SF-25C Falke self-launching motorised glider, otherwise known as the Venture T2. The school operated the Venture for just five years until 1991 when the Grob G109B Vigilant T1 motorised glider entered RAF service. Initially the school received three aircraft, however rationalisation and restructuring within the Air Cadet Organisation has meant that the unit currently has just two aircraft on charge.

In 1992, the trustees of the MacRobert's Trust attended a naming ceremony at RAF Kinloss, where their three aircraft were named 'Lady MacRobert', 'Sir Iain' and 'Sir Roderic'. In 2005, changes in command structure resulted in 663 VGS being renamed a Volunteer Gliding Squadron. The squadron is currently under the command of Squadron Leader Malcolm Parsons RAF VR(T), an A2 Gliding Instructor, and a former photographic interpreter.

Responsibility - *No. 663 VGS currently has a total of thirteen staff members, including three commissioned officer instructors. Geographically, the squadron looks after the largest region within the Air Cadet Organisation, which includes Stornoway and Wick in the north and as far south as Stonehaven.*

Flight Staff Cadet Grant Linklater shares his experience of his Gliding Scholarship.

"I was made to feel very welcome by all the staff when, as a young 16-year-old cadet, I arrived at 663 VGS to start my Gliding Scholarship. Flying safety is paramount, and I was given a full health and safety brief about the premises, the airfield and the aircraft. Staff instructors provided briefs and lectures on important exercises and this certainly helped the flying training. I felt at home on the squadron throughout the course because the atmosphere was always relaxed.

Once I had completed the required training and passed the first solo exam to a high standard, I had to complete a final check-flight to assess my ability to fly the aircraft correctly and safely. This comprised a few circuits flown under supervision and a few simulated engine failures. Fortunately the instructor deemed that I was competent and safe to fly solo. As he climbed out of the cockpit and closed the canopy behind him, I had never felt so isolated and nervous. Reality struck me that the whole of the next flight was all up to me and nobody else. I completed the checks as instructed. Had I done them correctly? Was there something wrong with the aircraft that I did not know about? Such questions disappeared from my thoughts as quickly as they were formed!"

cont'd page 134

Courses - There are three main gliding courses available in the Air Training Corps – Gliding Induction Courses (GIC), Gliding Scholarship (GS) and Advanced Glider Training (AGT). The GIC comprises three one-day courses, each teaching a different flying principal – Pitch, Roll and Yaw. From the age of 16, a cadet can apply for a GS, and in the case of the VGSs operating the Vigilant T1 motorised glider, this comprises eight flying hours of tuition. If the cadet shows promise, he or she may then complete a further two flying hours and subsequently perform a first solo flight and be awarded his or her silver wings. Those cadets who show exceptional aptitude may then progress onto their AGT, which comprises a further five hours of flying training, after which time they are awarded their gold wings. Usually these cadets will be enrolled as Flight Staff Cadets (FSCs) where further training to instructor categories is possible.

Control - The squadron operates mainly at weekends, with its modern launch control caravan being positioned on RAF Kinloss's disused cross-runway. No. 663 VGS completed 96% of their flying taskings in the period May 2007 to May 2008, which represents a little over 431 flying hours completed.

Capable - Flight duration is usually 20 to 30 minutes long, depending on what stage of training the cadet is at. RAF Kinloss's active 7,500ft (2,284m) runway is used for take-off and landing.

Cockpit - With a wingspan of 57ft (17.4 m), the Grob G109B Vigilant T1 is slightly smaller than its engineless Viking T1 counterpart. Powered by a single Grob 2500E1 horizontally opposed four-cylinder, air-cooled engine, the Vigilant is capable of a maximum speed of 130 knots.

cont'd from page 132

"Out on the landing strip, I lined up, applied full power and guided the aircraft into a perfect autumn afternoon. As the aircraft slowly clambered into the air, my thoughts were of disbelief "I cannot believe the Air Cadets are allowing me to do this!" As my confidence rose, I felt extremely happy. This was something I had dreamt of doing since before I joined the Air Cadet Organisation (ACO) three years previously. Now that dream, that crazy fantasy, was reality.

The flight seemed to end as quickly as it had started, with in my opinion, the best landing I had ever produced. As I taxied back to the glider caravan, I had a big smile on my face. Once the engine was shut down, an enormous sense of achievement, satisfaction and pride came over me. Feelings that remain with me each time I think about my first solo flight.

Taking an ACO Gliding Scholarship provided an unforgettable experience. The quality of the flying tuition received was brilliant and the atmosphere was down to earth and welcoming. I would strongly recommend this course to every member of the ACO. It was the most challenging and rewarding experience I have ever undertaken."

Taxi - The Vigilant is operated more like a light aircraft than a conventional glider. It taxies, takes off and climbs using the engine but can be used as a glider by switching the engine to idle, or even turning off the engine at the required height.

Fleet - The Air Cadet Organisation (ACO) has a fleet of 64 Vigilant T1s on strength, divided amongst 17 VGSs up and down the UK. The Air Cadet Central Gliding School (ACCGS) at Syerston, Nottinghamshire, also uses the type to train VGS instructors. No. 663 VGS is the only unit to operate the type in Scotland and currently has two aircraft on strength.

East of Scotland Universities' Air Squadron / 12 AEF

Cuide Laidire - *Together stronger*

Base: RAF Leuchars, Fife   **Aircraft:** Tutor

The East of Scotland Universities' Air Squadron (ESUAS) was formed after the amalgamation of East Lowlands UAS and Aberdeen, Dundee & St Andrews UAS in 2003. The roots of these University Air Squadrons date back from the mid 1920s when the first units were formed to provide university students with flying training. The first UAS on the East Coast of Scotland was formed in January 1941 and initial equipment consisted of the de Havilland Tiger Moth. Chipmunk T10s replaced the Tiger Moths in 1950 and were supplemented with Harvards for advance flying training. In 1975 the Chipmunks were replaced by Scottish Aviation Bulldog T1s which were subsequently replaced by Grob G115E Tutors in May 2000.

East Lowlands Universities' Air Squadron (ELUAS) was formed on 1 January 1969 from the amalgamation of Edinburgh University and St Andrews University Air Squadrons and operated out of Turnhouse, Midlothian. With the closure of RAF Turnhouse in March 1996, ELUAS moved its flying base to RAF Leuchars where it pooled its aircraft, engineering and accommodation with Aberdeen, Dundee and St Andrews Universities' Air Squadron and 12 AEF.

Aberdeen, Dundee and St Andrews Universities' Air Squadron was formed on 3 October 1981 following the amalgamation of Aberdeen UAS and St Andrews and Dundee UAS at RAF Leuchars. Aberdeen UAS was formed at Dyce, Aberdeenshire, on 23 January 1941 but moved to Leuchars in December 1980 due to the increased North Sea oil-related air traffic at Dyce.

ESUAS draws its members from students studying at universities in Aberdeen, Dundee, St Andrews and Edinburgh. The primary role of each UAS is to provide basic flying training and every student is offered 10 hours of flying per year. Students are encouraged to learn to fly the Tutor following a flying syllabus. This takes about three years in which about 30 flying hours are accumulated. Adventure training is another important role of the UAS. Free-fall parachuting, skiing, scuba-diving, kayaking and mountaineering are just as few of the activities used to engage in leadership training, team building and personal development.

Depart - *A Grob 115E Tutor, using callsign 'Claymore 1', climbs out from Runway 09 at RAF Leuchars en route to Angus. Two other resident aircraft types, the Tornado F3, seen here taxiing back to the 43 Squadron flight line in typical 'swept' configuration, and the Gazelle AH1 operated by 3 Flight, Army Air Corps (Volunteers). The latter now operate from 43(F) Squadron's former home in the Northern HAS complex.*

Outbound - *Built almost entirely from composite materials, including 96% carbon-fibre, the RAF's Grob G115E Tutors are powered by a single 180 horsepower Textron-Lycoming engine, with a top speed of 184 knots.*

Vista *- Much of RAF Leuchars is visible in this shot, as 'Claymore 1' is about to turn finals for Runway 09. East of Scotland Universities' Air Squadron came into being in 2003, after the amalgamation of two separate units – Aberdeen, Dundee & St Andrews Universities' Air Squadron and East Lowlands Universities' Air Squadron.*

Maintain - The RAF's Tutor fleet is owned and maintained by the VT Group under a Private Finance Initiative contract, operating a total of 99 aircraft for 14 University Air Squadrons throughout the UK.

Opposite
Patchwork - All University Air Squadrons and their embedded Air Experienced Flights are now part of 1 Elementary Flying Training School. Many of the aircraft wear the parent unit's crest comprising a tiger moth above a chrysalis. This aircraft is seen flying over South Angus.

Topside - No.12 Air Experience Flight (AEF) provides flying experience for Air Cadets from the East of Scotland. The AEF is staffed by one full-time Senior Instructional Officer and up to 20 part-time ex-regular pilots. Air Training Corps Wings from Edinburgh, Aberdeen and Dundee fly from RAF Leuchars at weekends using ESUAS aircraft.

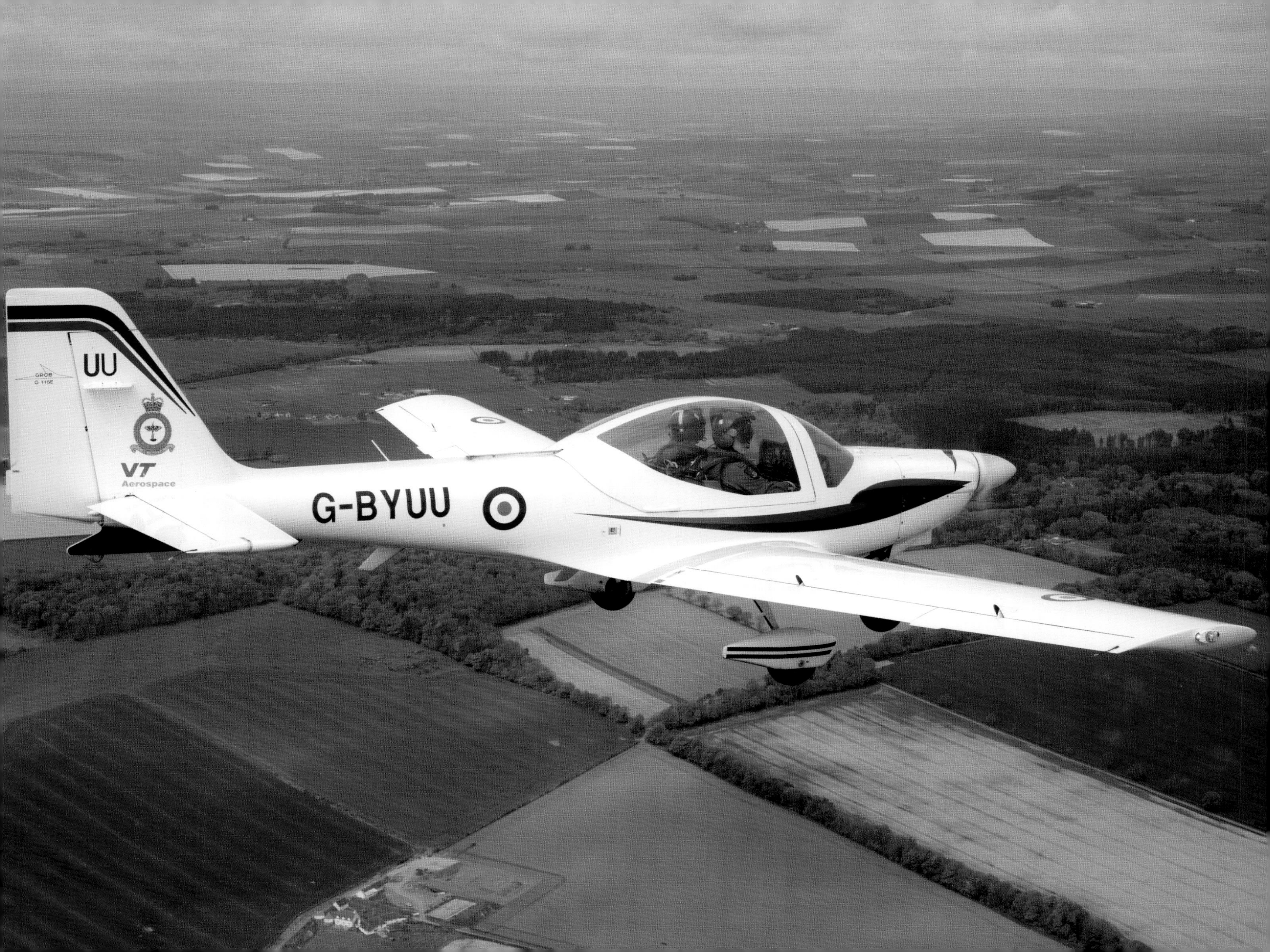

UU
GROB
G 115E
VT
Aerospace
G-BYUU

Universities of Glasgow & Strathclyde Air Squadron / 4 AEF

In Utrumque Paratus - Prepared for either event

Base: Glasgow International Airport, Renfrewshire   **Aircraft:** Tutor

The squadron was formed on 13 January 1941, and during World War Two was actively engaged in pre-entry training of students for the Royal Air Force. By the end of hostilities some 400 members had entered the service in various aircrew categories, though the squadron did not operate aircraft during this period. In 1946 the RAF Volunteer Reserve was re-organised and the squadron was equipped with Tiger Moths and Magisters.

In September 1950 these aircraft were replaced by Chipmunks, which remained in service for 25 years until 1974 when the squadron received the Scottish Aviation Bulldog T1. In March 2000 Grob G115E Tutors replaced the Bulldogs. Flying was initially carried out from Royal Naval Air Station Abbotsinch (HMS Sanderling), now Glasgow Airport.

In 1950 the airfield runway was re-laid and the squadron moved to Scone Airfield at Perth, some 70 miles (113km) from Glasgow, where the squadron remained until returning to Glasgow Airport in 1969. In 1965 the Royal College of Science and Technology became Strathclyde University and the unit was renamed the Universities of Glasgow and Strathclyde Air Squadron (UGSAS). More recently, students of the University of the West of Scotland, Glasgow Caledonian University and the Glasgow School of Art have become eligible for squadron membership.

In April 1996 the squadron became the parent of 4 Air Experience Flight. The squadron badge, approved in 1948, bears the motto, In Utrumque Paratus, which means 'Prepared for either event', with the link between the sword of war and the dove of peace featuring in the squadron badge.

Checks - Students enrolled into the University Air Squadron are afforded 10 hours of free flying per year. Should the student wish to use this time to learn to fly, he or she will be provided with expert tuition from a Qualified Flying Instructor (QFI). The flying syllabus is approximately 30 hours long, comprising general handling, instrument flying and basic navigation, culminating in a first solo flight after 10 hours of tuition. Further training, including aerobatics and formation flying, is available to those who finish the syllabus. Here a young student prepares himself for a solo flight in one of the squadron's Tutors.

Groundwork - *Joining a UAS is often seen as a perfect introduction to a career in the RAF. Many military aviators began their careers in aviation as a member of a UAS or Air Cadet Organisation. The young Officer Cadet seen here strapping himself into the cockpit is due to begin his initial officer training at RAF Cranwell, Lincolnshire, in late 2008, after which he can move on to an Elementary Flying Training course in the RAF.*

Embedded with the Universities of Glasgow and Strathclyde Air Squadron is 4 Air Experience Flight (AEF). Its main task is to provide members of the Air Cadet Organisation with an opportunity to fly in the Grob G115E Tutor. Each cadet, whether a member of the Air Training Corps (ATC) or the RAF section of the Combined Cadet Force (CCF) will get the opportunity to fly with an AEF at least once a year. A flight lasts approximately 25 minutes and the cadet can choose what he or she would like to do. Usually, cadets who have never flown in a light aircraft before will be shown some basic handling of the aircraft and get to enjoy the view from the cockpit. More experienced cadets, and those who have flown before, might want to opt for some aerobatics or even fly the aircraft themselves!

Links - *Demonstrating the affiliation between the Universities of Glasgow & Strathclyde Air Squadron and 602 (City of Glasgow) Squadron, Royal Auxiliary Air Force, some of the unit's Tutors have been adorned with a small 602 Squadron badge and 'fighter bar' style tartan. These are visible on the tail and aft of the aircraft registration.*

Honour - *A two-ship formation of the squadron's Tutors approaches the River Clyde in Glasgow. January 2008 saw the re-organisation of the squadron into two flights, named 'Clydesdale' and 'MacIntyre'. The names were given in honour of two of 602 (City of Glasgow) Squadron's former pioneering aviators – the Marquis of Douglas & Clydesdale (later to become the 14th Duke of Hamilton) who commanded the squadron between 1927 and 1936, and Flight Lieutenant David MacIntyre. Both had the distinction of being the first men ever to fly over Mount Everest in the Himalayas.*

The staff of 4 AEF consists of seven experienced flying instructors (all volunteers) who aim to fly 16 cadets per day. With two aircraft available, eight cadets fly in the morning and the other eight will get airborne in the afternoon, weather and aircraft serviceability permitting. When they arrive at the AEF, cadets will be shown a 15 minute long safety video about the Tutor aircraft and how to operate the parachute in case of an emergency.

The cadets are then kitted out with a flight suit and a helmet. Each cadet walks out to an aircraft with a pilot who assists with the straps and intercom leads. Once complete, the canopy is closed, the engine started and the aircraft taxies out for take off for a 25 minute flight. Let the fun begin! That's what air experience flights are all about - to promote and encourage an interest in aviation and the Royal Air Force.

Transition - *The Grob Tutor has side-by-side seating, but unlike its predecessor, the Scottish Aviation Bulldog, the primary flight instruments are now situated on the right hand side of the cockpit. This is enormously beneficial to the would-be RAF fast jet pilot because the student can fly the aircraft from the right-hand seat with a right-hand stick and a left-hand throttle - similar to a fast jet.*

Exercises & Air Shows

Nitex - Held annually in late winter at RAF Kinloss, the Night Tactical Leadership Training (NTLT) course is intended to develop the leadership skills of the RAF's front line aircrew within a controlled theatre of operations, specifically in a night-time environment. Approximately 40 fixed-wing aircraft and helicopters take part in the two-week long exercise, including the RAF's latest fighter aircraft, the Eurofighter Typhoon F2, flown by 3(F) Squadron. The exercise is planned and coordinated from pseudo-dedicated facilities within a hangar at RAF Kinloss, and is run by the Air Warfare Centre based at RAF Waddington in Lincolnshire. To avoid repetitive noise footprints over populated areas, NTLT missions are flown as far afield as the Isle of Skye and Newcastle.

Opposite
Gloamin' - The Typhoon FGR4 is the multi-role variant of the RAF's fourth generation fighter, and recently took part in large force exercises for the first time. This 11 Squadron example is pictured on final approach into RAF Kinloss. The Moray base is host to the two-week operational flying phase of the Combined Qualified Weapons Instructor (CQWI) course, which is the culmination of six months of training for the RAF's potential weapons instructors.

Rapid - Primarily used to deploy troops who act as the Land Component's 'Raid Force', several helicopters from the RAF's Support Helicopter Force take part in the NTLT exercise, including Chinook HC2s from RAF Odiham in Hampshire.

Force - A pilot's eye view of the Visiting Aircraft Servicing Section ramp at RAF Kinloss during a Combined Qualified Weapons Instructor (CQWI) course with Hawk T1As, Tornado F3s, Tornado GR4s and Falcon 20s parked on the flight line.

Opposite (top)
Opposition - Augmenting Tornado F3s and Typhoon F2s in the air defence role are Hawk T1As of 19(R) Squadron, seen here departing RAF Leuchars as a three-ship formation. Leuchars hosted the two week operational flying phase of the CQWI exercises before the exercise was moved to RAF Kinloss, Moray in 2006. Three F-15C Eagles of the 493rd Fighter Squadron (FS), part of the 48th Fighter Wing, based at RAF Lakenheath, Suffolk, can be seen in the background, waiting for their departure clearance. The 493rd FS often provides 'Red Air' or enemy fighter opposition for CQWI strike packages.

Opposite (bottom)
Sweep - Typhoon F2s and FGR4s from 11 Squadron taxi to the Kinloss runway at the start of a CQWI mission. Acting as fighter escorts for a strike package of Tornado GR4s, the Typhoons sweep airspace for enemy 'Red Air' fighters to enable Tornado GR4s to reach their designated target.

Raptor - Ground crews from II(AC) Squadron undertake RAPTOR (Reconnaissance Airborne Pod for Tornado) familiarisation training at RAF Kinloss between CQWI sorties. RAPTOR is a stand-off electro-optical and infrared, long-range oblique-photography pod specifically carried by the Tornado GR4. The images can be displayed in-cockpit during flight or transmitted instantly to analysts on the ground for dissemination. No. II(AC) Squadron based at RAF Marham, Norfolk is the lead RAPTOR unit within the Tornado GR4 Force.

Hereward *- The large areas of unrestricted airspace and uninhabited swathes of the Scottish Highlands make RAF Kinloss the ideal location from which to launch CQWI strike packages totalling up to 40 aircraft. This II(AC) Squadron Tornado GR4 wears special markings applied to celebrate the unit's 90th Anniversary.*

Albert - Low flying training exercises are regularly undertaken in designated areas of the UK by a variety of the RAF's frontline types, the largest of those being the Lockheed Hercules based at RAF Lyneham, Wiltshire.

Deck - Current overseas operations frequently dictate the need for low level flying in a hostile environment. In order to do this successfully, aircrews require specialist training gained through the use of the UK Low Flying System. Here, a Hawk T1 of 19(R) Squadron, based at RAF Valley, Anglesey, transits through the valleys of the Scottish Borders.

Warrior *- Held twice a year around the coastline and skies of Scotland, Exercise Joint Warrior is designed to increase the interoperability between coalition and NATO allies in a maritime environment. A combined force of around 50 land and carrier-based aircraft take part, many from overseas nations operating from RAF Kinloss and RAF Lossiemouth. Much of the flying takes place in the Highlands, often at low-level, with resident Tornado GR4s from RAF Lossiemouth's 140 Expeditionary Air Wing (EAW) providing a significant number of sorties throughout the two-week long exercise.*

Excellence - *Renowned the world over, The Red Arrows are ambassadors for the Royal Air Force and the United Kingdom as a whole. Flying nine Hawk T1 advanced trainers, the team continues to thrill audiences wherever they go.*

Spirit - *No. 230 Squadron take their membership of the NATO Tiger Meet Association seriously. For the 2005 meet, the squadron painted one of its Puma HC1s in a flamboyant tiger colour scheme. The aircraft participated in a number of air shows that year, including Arbroath's Seafront Spectacular.*

Remember - On Sunday the 15th of September 1940, the Royal Air Force fought its last major engagement of the Battle of Britain, effectively ending one of the most significant periods of World War Two. Subsequent raids by the Luftwaffe were on a much-reduced scale. Consequently, the 15th of September is celebrated each year as Battle of Britain Day. RAF Leuchars has held an annual airshow on the Saturday closest to this date since 1945. Now a multi-national event, it is the largest of its kind held in Scotland, and regularly attracts 50,000 people. As well as having the honour of being the oldest flying station in the Royal Air Force, Leuchars is now the only operational station to hold an airshow to specifically commemorate the Battle of Britain. One of its highlights is the display by the Hurricane, Lancaster and Spitfire of the RAF's Battle of Britain Memorial Flight based at Coningsby, Lincolnshire. A reminder to all of the sacrifices made by so many during World War Two.

Opposite (middle)
Demo - The RAF Role Demonstration showcases some of the RAF's current front line assets in a realistic battlefield scenario. Pyrotechnic effects are used to demonstrate fire power, as can be seen here during a mock airfield attack by a Tornado GR4 from 12(B) Squadron at Leuchars Airshow.

Royal Air Force Benevolent Fund

RAF Benevolent Fund Scotland, 20 Queen Street, Edinburgh, EH2 1JX - Tel: 0131 225 6421

The Royal Air Force Benevolent Fund was formed one year after the formation of the Royal Air Force and celebrates its 90th Anniversary in 2009. It has operated from its Scottish base in the heart of Edinburgh for over 60 years. With large RAF Stations such as Kinloss, Leuchars and Lossiemouth, and smaller units at Benbecula, Buchan, Prestwick and Tain, there are almost 8,000 RAF personnel serving in Scotland with their immediate families and dependants. There are also many other retired members of service making up the wider 'RAF family' in Scotland. With current plans to base the Typhoon at RAF Leuchars, the Nimrod MRA4 at RAF Kinloss and the Joint Strike Fighter at RAF Lossiemouth, there are very sound reasons to maintain a solid Benevolent Fund base in Scotland.

Leased by the MacRobert's Trust, the Benevolent Fund managed Alastrean House in Tarland, Aberdeenshire, as an RAF care home for many years.

Although the home is now operated by Balhousie Care, the Fund continues to support a number of residents who have a Royal Air Force connection. One of these residents is Mina Tedder, daughter of the late Lord Tedder, Chief of the Air Staff between 1946 and 1950. Mina loves Alastrean House where she enjoys a quality of life in a grand setting. She often drives to the local village on her electric scooter and she is a bit of an expert when it comes to growing cherry tomatoes in the greenhouse!

Bill Beattie is another resident in Alastrean House. Bill was 90 years of age the day before the RAF celebrated its 90th birthday on 1st April 2008. He served in the RAF during World War Two as a radio and telecommunications expert and continues practicing his skills to this day by keeping in contact with other morse code operators around the world.

The Benevolent Fund engages closely with Royal Air Force personnel – after all, it is their charity. The Fund is there to support those of the wider RAF family who might fall on hard times perhaps through sickness, ill health, poverty or disability. Serving RAF personnel are also great at supporting the Fund, not only by contributing half a day's pay on an annual basis, but some may take part in a sponsored event to raise funds. Last year for example, RAF Leuchars-based No. 56(R) Squadron, otherwise known as the "Firebirds", raised £50,000 for the Fund by staging the very successful "Firebirds Invitational" – a two-day event which comprised golf at Gleneagles, rally car driving and a military skills competition.

Each year the Benevolent Fund helps a wide range of people who have fallen on hard times. Increasingly this often includes families who have been left following the loss of husbands and fathers on active service. Bob Kemp, Director of the Benevolent Fund in Scotland, said; "This is the debt we owe. The Kinloss-based Nimrod lost over Afghanistan, left many families, some with young children, without a father or husband. The Fund is there to ensure that that dependants and widows are looked after should they fall on hard times".

RAFBF

THE HEART
OF THE RAF FAMILY

If you would like to support the Fund in Scotland, please contact Bob Kemp at:

RAF Benevolent Fund
20 Queen Street
Edinburgh EH2 1JX
Tel: 0131 225 6421

"Thank you for your support"

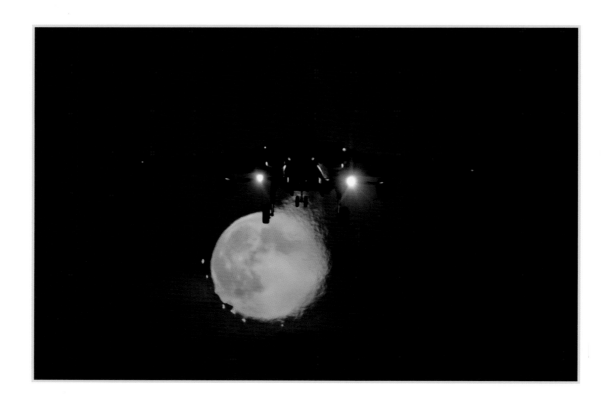